<u>BMAT Revision Guides For</u>
<u>Sections 1, 2 & 3</u>

- In Depth Analysis of Section 1 Questions

- 70+ Topics Covered for Section 2

- Section 3 Tips & Tricks with 10 Sample Essays

Table of Contents

How To Use This Book?

Read through the guides given in this book at least once. There are 140 pages in this book and if you read only 10 pages a day, it will only take 14 days for you to complete this book.

Read through all of the guides on Sections 1 & 3. They are very important and will assist you whilst you are practising past papers.

There are a lot of guides on Section 2. It is understandable if you are unable to complete all guides. However, try your best!

There are some topics in Section 2, which are very important, and you should go through them at least once. This because questions from these topics are frequent. Here is the list:

Biology	Chemistry	Physics	Maths
Initiation of Heartbeat	Balancing Equations	Circuits	Rearranging
Enzymes	Reactivity Series	Force and Free Fall	Factorisation and Splitting the Middle Term
Meiosis	Oxidation Numbers	Energy	Surds
Mitosis	Moles	Momentum	Simultaneous Equations
Digestive System	Molar Ratios	Waves	n^{th} Term and Linear Sequences
Homeostasis	Empirical Formula	Types of Radiation	Pythagoras Theorem
Hormones	Percentage Yield	Half-Life	Probability
Reflex Arc	Group Chemistry	Nuclear Fusion & Fission	
Inheritance		Moments	

Try and understand these topics before you revise anything else, as questions from these topics come up more often than questions from any other topics.

Obviously, do not disregard the other topics!

As you are going through this book, do past papers as well. This will help you to keep a balance between obtaining knowledge and practising.

Revise well and Good Luck!

Preparation for Section 1

1) Practise! Practise! Practise! Please do not think that 2-3 past papers are enough to be fully ready for the exam. I am not saying that you have to do all past papers but if you have time to prepare, do as many past papers as you can.

2) Past Papers are the best resources you can get for the BMAT. Try your best to do as many as you can **under exam conditions!**

3) 1 question takes around 1 minute 40 seconds to do. Aim for this whilst doing each question.

4) Time yourself from the very first day and be strict about it! Do not be lenient and give yourself extra time because you will not get any in the real exam.

5) Every time you attempt a past paper, do the shorter, easier questions first. All questions are worth 1 mark. I personally believe that critical thinking questions are easier than data analysis and spatial awareness questions. However, every person is different, and you may think the opposite. Please identify the types of questions you are good at and do those first.

6) I highly suggest you leave the Spatial Awareness questions until the end and only attempt them when you have time left after you have completed other questions. These questions usually cost students a lot of time, which they can use to solve easier questions. There is no specific method to solve Spatial Awareness questions and they will give you ones that are different from the past paper questions.

7) Try not to do past paper questions online. It would be ideal to print out the past papers so you can underline important parts of texts and do calculations on the question paper. This helps you to get a real feel of the exam.

8) You should know that you are given an answer sheet in which you have to shade the correct option. Remember to print this out as well together with your past paper.
NOTE: The response sheet for each past paper is different. So please ensure that print out the correct response sheet.
E.g. If you print out the 2010 past paper, you must print out the 2010 answer sheets. You cannot use the 2009 response sheet for the 2010 past paper.

9) Lastly, do not forget to shade an answer for every question!

Section 1: Critical Thinking

Critical Thinking

1) 4 types of questions:

- Conclusion
- Assumption
- Flaws
- Strengthen/Weaken

Please read the lessons in which I discuss each of the four types of critical thinking questions.

2) Don't read the long bit of text first! Read the main question first: 'e.g. what is the main conclusion?' or "what is the assumption?' this will save A LOT of time. Some texts can take 1 or 2 minutes to understand which is not ideal.

3) By reading the question first, you will have an idea of what to look for in the passage.

4) Underline the sentence, which summarises or concludes the passage. This sentence is NOT necessarily the last sentence of the text, although it often could be.

5) If you are asked to find the flaw, conclusion or assumption, this sentence will help you to arrive at your answer.

6) Work out what the answer is and use the process of elimination to discard all options, which are incorrect.

7) If you are confused between two or three options, skim through the passage quickly and look for certain keywords. The answer is often the option, which has the keywords the passage has, although you must ensure whether or not that option is potentially the answer.

Conclusion Questions

A **conclusion** is the summing-up of an argument or text.

In conclusion questions, you will be given piece(s) of text with lots of information. You will then be asked to select the statement, which correctly identifies the conclusion of the text.

Like any other critical thinking question, it is important that you read the question first instead of the text. This will save you time and allow you to obtain the correct answer.

Usually (not always), the conclusion could the last line of the text. However, this is not necessary.

Procedure:

1) Look at the question to see what is asked of you but do not look at the options provided.

2) **Skim** through the text to get an idea of what the text is saying.

3) Try and arrive at an answer in your head without looking at the options. By not looking at the options first and coming up with your answer, you are able to clear any confusion that you may have between two options.

4) Then look at the options and **eliminate** those, which are either irrelevant or completely incorrect.

5) If you successfully managed to eliminate all options but one, then the one remaining should be the answer.

6) If you are confused between two options, just quickly skim through the text again and look for relevant, **keywords**, which may be in one option but not in the other.

Example: (Past Paper 2011 Section 1 Question 26)

Try solving this question on your own first using the method mentioned above. Make sure and time yourself! Ideally, you should be spending 1 minute 30 seconds on each question.

Solution:

A – Wrong
Having a gravity similar to Earth is not a sufficient enough condition for supporting life.

B – Wrong
Liquid water being able to form oceans, lakes and rivers is not a sufficient enough condition for supporting life.

C – Correct
This is correct because of the line "planets like this **must** be really common".

D – Wrong
"is probably **in the order of** 10 or 20 per cent" is different from "10 or 20 per cent of systems **have**."
This statement is too strong.

E – Wrong
The text says that "there could be" and not "there are". One word makes the whole difference. This statement is too strong.

Assumption Questions

An **assumption** is something, which is accepted as being true or certain to happen in the future, without any evidence.

The Procedure:

1) Firstly, identify the conclusion of the text.
2) Then ask yourself "Why?"
3) The answer to the question "Why?" will help you reach the assumption.

It may sound complicated but let us look at an example

Example:
Try and figure out what the assumption is in the following sentence:

> "**Carbon dioxide contributes to global warming. Therefore, we should limit carbon dioxide emissions**".

Conclusion: "We should limit carbon dioxide emissions."
Why? Because "Carbon dioxide contributes to global warming."

In the answer to the question "Why?" you need to realise that carbon dioxide contributes to global warming. Since we want to limit carbon dioxide emissions, we must also want to limit global warming. Therefore, global warming is a bad thing.

The assumption in the above sentence is that global warming is bad for us. Now, you may be wondering, well, global warming is obviously bad for us and that is a fact.
However, no matter how obvious it is, that is still the underlying assumption of the sentence above.

Example 2:

> "**I bought a lot of lottery tickets, so I have a higher chance of winning the lottery**".

Conclusion: "I have a higher chance of winning the lottery."
Why? Because "I bought a lot of lottery tickets."

There is a link between buying a lot of lottery tickets and a higher chance of winning the lottery.
Assumption: Buying more lottery tickets increases your chances of winning the lottery.

Using "Opposite Sentences"

I don't really know what to call this, but this method also helps us to identify assumptions. This helps to identify the assumption when we are confused between two given options.

The Procedure:

1) Identify the conclusion of the text.
2) Eliminate all the obvious, incorrect options.
3) Make the potential or possible options opposite. E.g. "You should exercise" would become "You should not exercise".
4) Fit the opposite, possible options into the text and see if it makes sense.

Example: (Past Paper 2015 Section 1 Q13)

Conclusion: For such influential people, there should not be a second chance.
Why? This would send out a wrong message to young people that such behaviour is acceptable.

Easy Eliminations:
1) A (only focuses on football fans whilst the text just uses football as an example)
2) B (depends on the nature of the crime)
3) C (Again, football is only used as an example in the text)
4) E is wrong because it is not an assumption.

Let us see now why D is the correct answer by using the opposite sentence.
D would become "The rights of the individual are less important than risks to society".

Opposite: Influential people such as footballers should not be allowed back into employment if they have served a prison sentence for serious crimes because it risks sending a message to young fans that such behaviour is acceptable. The rights of the individual are **more** important than risks to society.
This certainly does not make sense. If the rights of individuals are more important than risks to society then certainly, influential people should be allowed back into employment. Since this does not make sense and we make option B original again, it should make sense.

Original: Influential people such as footballers should not be allowed back into employment if they have served a prison sentence for serious crimes because it risks sending a message to young fans that such behaviour is acceptable. The rights of the individual are **less** important than risks to society. This certainly makes sense. Therefore, D is the correct answer.

Multiple Options
In these types of questions, you are given 2-3 sentences in which either, one is an assumption, two are assumptions or all are assumptions.

These types of questions are pretty difficult and they require a longer amount of time to answer.
However, you can still answer them using the methods described above.

Example: (Past Paper 2013 Section 1 Question 30)

Conclusion: "Wrinkled fingers are advantageous to us"
Why? "It gives human beings a better grip underwater"

Statement 1 (correct): The last line of the paragraph assumes that gripping objects underwater could be advantageous to us.

Statement 2 (wrong): Although this may be true, it is irrelevant to the argument made in the paragraph.

Statement 3 (correct): The fact that characteristics are termed advantageous means that they must have helped us in some way (been advantageous to us). Therefore, this is an assumption of the text. So, we can eliminate B.

So, D is the correct answer.

Flaw Questions

With regards to the BMAT, a flaw is a fault or inadequacy in an argument, which reduces the argument's effectiveness.
In simpler words, it means what is wrong with the argument made in the text?

There are many types of flaws that you can be presented within the exam.

1) Straw Man
2) False Dilemma
3) Ad Hominem
4) Generalisation
5) Circular Reasoning
6) Correlation is not Causation
7) Syllogisms
8) Tu Quoque
9) Slippery Slope

However, you do not need to go into detail about each type of flaw and learn their definition. We will discuss them to give you an idea of how you can identify the flaw of each argument.

Straw Man
This refers to giving the impression of refuting a person's argument while refuting the argument, which was not represented by the person in the first place.

Example:
Person A: Nation should not spend more money on the army and defence
Person B: No! We cannot leave the nation defenceless!

This means that Person A was straw-manned. Person A's argument was just to spend less money on defence whilst Person B represented A's argument in the wrong way. B made it seem that A's argument was: "We should remove the army and make the nation defenceless" which was not the case.

Slippery Slope
In this type of flaw, a small first step can lead to a chain of related events, which could result in significant, negative effects.
In simple words, if A happens, B will happen. If B happens, C will happen. If C happens, there will be some significant effects.

Example:
If more people get low marks in an exam, grade boundaries would become lower. If grade boundaries become lower, more incompetent students are likely to pass the exam with good grades. If more incompetent people enter university, we will have less incompetent professionals in different fields.

In the example, you can see how one event led to another.

False Dilemma
This is a fallacy based on an "either/or" type of argument. In this, two choices are presented and a claim is made that one is false and one is true.

Example:
Child to parent: You either buy this book for me or you think that I should not improve my reading skills.

Ad Hominem
In this, an argument is based on emotional appeal rather than logical appeal. One type of ad hominem

appeals to the emotions of the other person whilst the other type emotionally attacks the person's character.

Example:
A politician arguing that the opponent cannot possibly be a good choice for education because they have not gotten a degree.

Generalisation
When one makes a generalisation, they apply a belief to a larger population than they should, based on the information they have.

Example:
The first person you meet in a new country is rude so you tell your friends from another country that all people in this country are rude.

Circular Reasoning
In this, the proposition is supported by the premises, which in turn, are supported by the proposition. In simpler words, "X is true because Y is true and Y is true because X is true."

Example:
Piracy is wrong because it is against the law and it is against the law because it is wrong.

Tu Quoque
A Tu Quoque argument attacks a person by focusing on their past words or actions instead of their current arguments and claims.
Person A makes a claim.
Person B says that person A's past actions or claims are inconsistent with the truth of A's claim.
Therefore, A's claim is false.

Example:
A politician's speech about the misuse and dangers of drugs is attacked because there is a record of that politician using drugs before.

Correlation and Causation
Just because two things are correlated and usually occur together, that does not mean that one causes the other.

The phrase "correlation does not imply causation" is very popular and it implies that a correlation between two things does not mean that one thing causes the other.

Example:
Many people who drink tea are thin. Therefore, we should drink coffee to lose weight.
Argument: "We should drink coffee to lose weight."

This is clearly not true and hence the flaw is that the argument confuses correlation with causation.

Syllogisms
This is a very common type of flaw found in the BMAT.
It is better to explain this using a simple example.
Some A are B
Some B are C
Therefore, some A are C

Example:
Some books are black things
Some black things are televisions
Therefore some cats are televisions

Well, this is clearly not true.

14) E
The text just transitions from the hours spent on internet by teenagers to isolation and obesity. This indicates that the text is trying to suggest that excessive use of the internet is causing isolation and obesity.

A – Wrong
The text is not focused on the benefits of Internet. So A is irrelevant.

B – Wrong
The text is meant to focus only on teenagers who use the internet excessively.

C – Wrong
It does not assume parents can enforce stricter controls. It just states that parents must enforce stricter controls. There is a difference between assuming and advising.

D – Wrong
TV and computer games are irrelevant as the text is meant to focus only on internet.

E – Correct
This identifies the flaw which is the causal link made by the text between internet and isolation and obesity.

Strength/Weakness Questions

I personally find these questions usually easier than other critical thinking questions. In such questions, you are given a piece of text and 4-5 options. You are then supposed to choose which of the options either strengthens or weakens the argument made in the text.

Procedure:

1) Just like any other critical thinking question, your first step should be to **find the conclusion of the text**.

2) Then use the "Fact" test. In this test, we assume that each of the statements given to us as options is true. (I will explain this using an example)

3) Check which of the options strengthen or weaken the argument.

It sounds simple and to be honest, it is! Let us use an example.

Strengthen Example: (Past Paper 2010 Section 1 Question 28)

Conclusion: "...the name alone had influenced public opinion and prevent people from having sympathy for the child."
ONLY the name had influenced public opinion and nothing else.
We are given three statements in this question and our job is to identify those statements, which would strengthen the conclusion (or the argument made in the text). Let us analyse each statement using the Fact test.

1 – Correct
If the media had reported the child's background accurately, this would have reduced bias and hence ensure that there were not any other factors that influenced public opinion except the name.

2 – Wrong
If the newspaper called for the harshest possible punishment, then the name together with the newspaper's statement would have been the factors influencing public opinion. So, the name would not have been the ONLY factor influencing public opinion.

3 – Wrong
If this statement were true, then the newspaper's wording also would have influenced public opinion. So, the name would not have been the ONLY factor.

Weakness Example: (Past paper 2012 Section 1 Question 15)

Conclusion: "So parents of children with autism...using the sprays."

Our job is to identify the statement, which weakens the above conclusion. Let us use the Fact test to see which statement weakens the argument.

A – Wrong

If oxytocin causes feelings of envy, then this would mean that parents would be damaging their children's health. This, instead, strengthens the argument.

B – Wrong

This statement actually strengthens the argument as since there have been no scientific studies made, parents could potentially be damaging their children's health.

C – Correct

This is definitely correct. If levels of oxytocin are low in the sprays and it does not have any effect on children, then parents would not be damaging their children's health.

D – Wrong

The type of culture an individual lives in, is not directly relevant to the question.

E – Wrong

This strengthens the statement as such effects could cause damage to a child's health.

Section 1: Problem Solving Questions

Candidates often feel that problem-solving questions are the most difficult in Section 1. This is mainly because there is no specific method that you can use to solve them. Also, they come in many different types of varieties, as you can see from the list below.

Tips:

1) Types of Questions:

    1. PIN codes

    2. Diagram analysis (e.g. maps)

    3. Spatial Awareness

2) They can provide you with any sets of data and ask you analyse them. Again, practice is key, so try and do as many past papers as you can. Then check the worked solutions to see where you went wrong and rectify your mistake.

3) Section 1 Maths is very simple. Most questions only require the use of addition, subtraction, multiplication, division, fractions, percentages and ratios. Sometimes, simple probability questions may also be asked. Nothing more advanced will be asked of you. Of course, Section 2 Maths is a bit more difficult.

4) Like the critical thinking questions, look at the main questions first. Do not read the text or analyse the tables/graphs first.

5) Look at the options given before you do any calculations. This will give you an idea of what your answer should be.
E.g. if the options include 4, 6, 9 and 12, and you get an answer of 100; you know that you have done something wrong. Therefore, by looking at the answers first, you will get some idea about where you should start.

6) Do your calculations and solve the question. Brush up on your mental maths skills, as this will come in handy if you are running out of time.

7) I suggest you to not do the past paper questions online. Print out the past papers and do them under exam conditions. This will help to avoid any distractions and give you a real feel of the exam.

8) Each question requires different calculations and analysis. There is no specific method to solve these types of questions. Therefore, I suggest you practise as many past paper questions as you can under timed conditions.

PIN Codes (Forming Equations Technique)

These types of questions involve you having to find the numbers of PIN or a certain digit of a PIN. Usually, these questions take a long amount of time to answer, i.e., if you understand the information provided to you.

Let us look at an **Example: 2013 Section 1 Q14**. This is a past paper question so try and attempt it on your own first and then look at the following solution.

Solution:
Since four is the first digit, the second or third digits cannot be eight as 'e' comes before 'f' and the digits are in alphabetical order. It can also not be five as 'fo' in four comes after 'fi' in five.

They can neither be four nor zero, as all four digits must be different.
We can form an equation to match the information provided to us.
We know 4 has four letters
We know 0 has four letters
Let the 2nd digit be S
Let the 3rd digit be T

$4 + 0 + S + T = 8 +$ Number of letters in S + Number of letters in T S + $T = 4 +$ Number of letters in S + Number of letters in T

By placing in different digits, we get the answer to be 9 and 2.
Total number of letters in 9 and 2 = 4 + 3 = 7 So the answer is B

From this example, you can see by **forming equations**, we made it much easier for ourselves to find the correct answer. **This technique is not only useful for PIN code questions but for other questions too, when you are asked to find out an unknown value.**

Diagram Analysis
In these types of questions, you will be given a diagram such as a map of an area or a shape.

Example: (Past Paper 2015 Section 1 Question 23)

Solution:
Since the question says that the tourist visited 5 attractions by taking the shortest route, it makes sense to add the shortest routes possible from the hotel.
So, they definitely went to the Courts, which is 60m.
They then took the shortest route to the Fountain, which is 80m.
Then the Arch, which is 80m from the Fountain.
Then, the Castle, which is 90m from the Arch.
Then the Tower, which is 110m from the Castle.
Then back to the Hotel, which is 110m from the Tower.
Adding this up: 60 + 80 + 80 + 90 + 110 + 110 = 530m
So, the tourist did not go to the Palace.

To solve some questions, it is quicker to draw diagrams to reach the correct answer.

Example: 2018 Section 1 Q1

Solution:
The lines represent the bins whilst the circles represent the benches.

Within diagram analysis, I would also like to include the technique of **drawing Venn Diagrams**.

Example: There are only two sports options in a school, volleyball and football. Harry and Jessica do not play volleyball. Tom and Millie play volleyball. Tom and Gary play both volleyball and football. However, Morris does not play any of the mentioned sports. Harry does play one sport. Tammy plays one sport only. Which of the following statement(s) is/are true?

A) Jessica plays football
B) Tom plays both sports
C) Harry plays football
D) Millie plays volleyball only
E) Tammy plays volleyball

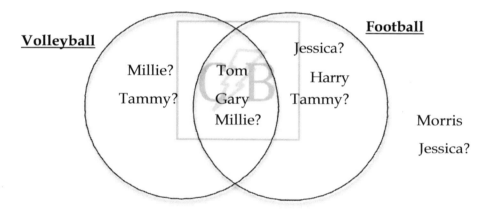

A) We know Jessica does not play volleyball. However, we are not given any more information about Jessica. So, we cannot be sure whether Jessica plays football or not. So, A is wrong.

B) Tom plays both volleyball and football. So, B is correct.

C) We know Harry does not play volleyball. But we know Harry plays one sport. Since there are only two sports in the school, Harry must be playing football. So, C is correct.

D) We know Millie plays volleyball. But we do not know whether she plays football or not. So, D is wrong.

E) We know Tammy plays one sport only. However, we do not know which sport. So, E is wrong.

Spatial Awareness

These types of questions involve a great deal of imagination, memory and cognitive ability. You may be given a net and be asked to select the cube it will form. In other questions, you may be given a die and then be asked to work out which number is on which face.

It is highly advisable you leave such questions for the last, as they are very time consuming.

However, there are some ways of preparing yourself for these types of questions.

1) Do past paper questions (obviously). For the first few questions that you come across, take your time. Try and remember what the shape would look like from different angles. If you forget the angles, try again and again till you remember. It only comes with practice.

2) Become familiar with how cubes are made from nets. Also, practise drawing cubes quickly on paper (for net questions)

Unfortunately, this is all. There are no formulae or specific methods to solve them. Again, do not linger on these questions during the exam. It is not worth it.

Section 1: Data Analysis

Data analysis questions are probably easier than problem solving questions. This is because you are given numbers and asked to work out a figure. You can follow a certain method to obtain the correct answer.

Tips:

1) Types of Questions:
    1. Numerical Questions
    2. Tables
    3. Graphs

2) Do not feel like you need to read through all the information given to you in the question. Look at the direct question first, i.e., the question that asks you to find the answer.

3) I suggest you then look at the options to find out what your answer could be. By looking at the options, you can get an idea about where you should be looking for the answer.

4) Look at the text, skim through it, find words similar to the ones in the question and options and then identify what the answer is.

5) Work on mental maths. Know your multiplication tables to at least 12x. This will be very helpful.

6) Know how to convert from decimals to percentages to fractions and vice-versa. Some questions can ask you to carry out such conversions. Also, be familiar with the concept of ratios.

7) Lastly, past papers questions under exam conditions!

I personally believe that data analysis questions are straightforward as the answer or information related to the answer is given to you in the text. It is just a matter of finding it/working it out.

Section 2 - Introduction

In Section 2, the questions are solely based on scientific knowledge. There is a specific way to solve each and every question.
Section 2 includes questions from Biology, Chemistry, Physics and Maths.
You have 30 minutes to solve 27 questions. This gives you just over 1 minute to solve each question. This is the reason why candidates often feel that section 2 is the toughest out of the three sections.

It is difficult to solve every question within the time limit, as some questions will be very long and difficult to understand. Therefore, it is advised that you attempt the easier questions first and then tackle the harder ones.

In this book, we will go through every topic from which questions can be asked in the exam. In order to save time, I advise you to skip the topics, which you are comfortable with and revise the ones you find difficult first. This way, you will be able to save valuable time. However, try your best to go through each topic at least once!

Biology - Active Transport

Active transport is the movement of molecules across a cell membrane from a region of lower concentration to a region of higher concentration.
Enzymes and energy assist active transport. Since it requires energy, it is known as an active process.
Since diffusion and osmosis do not require energy, they are known as passive processes.

Some Examples of Active Transport:

1) Carbohydrates are broken into smaller sugars like glucose. Glucose is absorbed by active transport into the villi of the small intestine.

2) Plants take up mineral salts such as nitrates into their plant root cells by active transport from the soil. This is because the concentration of nitrates is higher in the root cells and lower in the soil.

Biology - Diffusion and Osmosis

Diffusion

Diffusion is the movement of molecules from a region of higher concentration to a region of lower concentration.

Examples in our body:

1) In our lungs:

- Oxygen from alveoli to blood vessels

- Carbon dioxide from blood vessels to alveoli

2) In our tissues:

- Oxygen from capillaries to respiring cells

- Carbon dioxide from respiring cells to capillaries

- Glucose from capillaries to respiring cells

Osmosis

Osmosis is the movement of water molecules from a region of higher water concentration to a region of lower water concentration through a partially permeable membrane.

Osmosis occurs whenever there is movement of water molecules from a region of higher water concentration to a region of lower water concentration in our body.

Biology - Respiration

Respiration is a biochemical process, which releases energy using glucose so that all other chemical processes can happen.

NOTE: Respiration is not the same as breathing. The proper term for breathing is ventilation.

There are two types of respiration:

1) Aerobic respiration
2) Anaerobic respiration

Aerobic respiration

In aerobic respiration, glucose and oxygen react together in cells to produce carbon dioxide and water. This reaction releases energy. It is called aerobic because it requires oxygen from the air to work.

Glucose + oxygen -> carbon dioxide + water + (energy)

$$C_6H_{12}O_6 + 6O_2 \rightarrow 6CO_2 + 6H_2O$$

Most of the aerobic respiration occurs in the mitochondria.

Anaerobic respiration

During anaerobic respiration, the oxidation of glucose is incomplete. Therefore, anaerobic respiration releases much less energy.

Anaerobic respiration occurs in the absence of oxygen. Some organisms can respire without oxygen using anaerobic respiration. However, this is usually for short periods of time.

In **animals**, glucose in muscle is converted to lactic acid.
Glucose $\rightarrow$ lactic acid + (energy)

In **yeast**, glucose is converted to ethanol and carbon dioxide. This is also known as fermentation.
Glucose $\rightarrow$ ethanol + carbon dioxide + (energy)

Comparison of Aerobic and Anaerobic Respiration in Animals

	Aerobic Respiration	Anaerobic Respiration
Requires Oxygen?	Yes	No
Needs Glucose	Yes	Yes
Products	Carbon dioxide and water	Lactic acid
Energy released	More energy per glucose molecule	Less energy per glucose molecule

Biology - Exhalation and Inhalation

You may be asked about the aspects of processes of inhalation and exhalation.

Inhalation is breathing in
Exhalation is breathing out

Inhalation

1. Lungs move upward and outward
2. Diaphragm contacts and flattens
3. Intercostal muscles contract
4. Ribs move upward and outward
5. Volume inside the thoracic cavity increases
6. Pressure inside the thoracic cavity decreases
7. Air rushes into the lungs

Exhalation

1. Lungs move downward and inward
2. The diaphragm relaxes and curves upwards
3. Intercostal muscles relax
4. Ribs move downward and inward
5. Volume inside the thoracic cavity decreases
6. Pressure inside the thoracic cavity increases
7. Air rushes out of the lungs

Gas	Inhaled Air	Exhaled Air
Oxygen	21%	16%
Carbon dioxide	0.03%	4%
Nitrogen	78%	78%

Biology - Alveoli

An alveolus (plural: alveoli) is a tiny air sac of the lung. This is the site of gas exchange. They are located at the ends of the air passageways in the lungs.

Mechanism:

Air enters the lungs during inhalation. This air has a high concentration of oxygen. This oxygen-rich air enters the alveolus.
The concentration of oxygen is higher in the alveolus than in the red blood cells. Therefore, the oxygen diffuses into the blood of the capillary running near the alveolus.
The concentration of carbon dioxide is higher in the blood than in the alveolus. Therefore, carbon dioxide diffuses from the capillary into the alveolus.
Carbon dioxide is then removed from the body during exhalation.

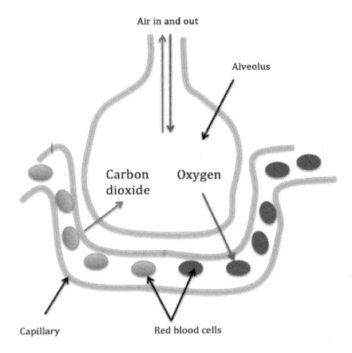

The lighter coloured red blood cells represent deoxygenated blood and the darker red blood cells represent the oxygenated blood.

Alveoli are adapted for their function. They are only one-cell thick and allow easy exchange of gases, as the diffusion distance is very short.
Also, an average human lung has approximately 480 million alveoli and a large capillary network surrounds these alveoli. This allows maximum gas exchange, as there is a large surface area.

NOTE: Emphysema is a condition in which air sacs (alveoli) of the lungs are damaged and enlarged.

Biology - ATP

ATP is the acronym for the nucleotide <u>A</u>denosine <u>T</u>ri-<u>P</u>hosphate.

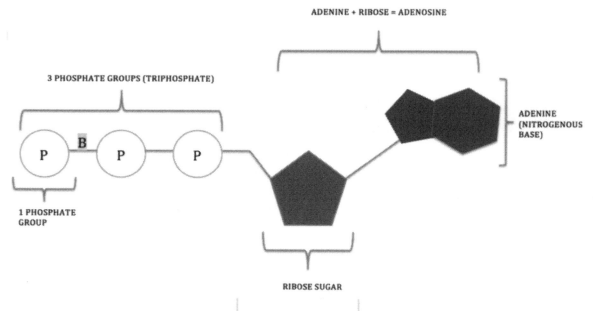

ATP consists of:
- A ribose sugar
- Three phosphate groups
- Adenine (a nitrogenous base)

ATP is considered to be a major energy currency of the cell. It is used for all reactions in all cells.

Properties of ATP:
- ATP is easily soluble
- Easily transported across membranes
- Release energy efficiently
- Only requires one enzyme (ATP synthase) to hydrolyse it
- Energy is released in small, useable amounts

Uses of ATP:
- Mechanical work (i.e. muscle contraction)
- Active Transport of molecules and ions
- Biosynthesis (building up complex molecules from simple molecules)

How is energy released from ATP?
A single enzyme known as ATP synthase hydrolyses or breaks the bond between the last and middle phosphate group (shown B on the diagram above). This releases energy in useable amounts, so little energy is wasted as heat.

How is ATP generated?
ATP is easily reformed by phosphorylation when a phosphate group is added to ADP (Adenosine Di-Phosphate) by condensation reaction. However, you do not need to know much more on ATP. You will learn more about Chemiosmosis in Year 13.

Biology - Circulatory System

The circulatory system circulates blood around the body.
It consists of:
- Blood
- Heart
- Blood vessels

Blood

The blood is made up of:
- Plasma (liquid part) which is made up of water, salts and protein
- Red blood cells (erythrocytes)
- White blood cells (leukocytes)
- Platelets

Blood acts as a transport system of our body, carrying oxygen in red blood cells and other nutrients in plasma.
It also plays a role in our immunity as it consists of white blood cells.

Heart

The heart is an organ made up of cardiac muscle. It contains four chambers:
- Right atrium
- Left atrium
- Right Ventricle
- Left Ventricle

The right side of the heart carries deoxygenated blood whilst the left side of the heart carries oxygenated blood.
A wall called septum separates the right and left sides of the heart.

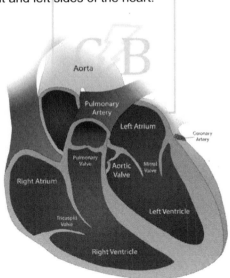

The heart also has valves to prevent backflow of blood.
- The tricuspid valve prevents backflow of blood from the right ventricle to right atrium.
- The mitral valve prevents backflow of blood from the left ventricle to left atrium.
- The pulmonary valve prevents backflow of blood from the pulmonary artery to the right ventricle.
- The aortic valve prevents backflow of blood from Aorta to left ventricle.

Blood Vessels

There are three types of blood vessels:
- Arteries
- Veins
- Capillaries

Arteries
- Arteries carry blood away from the heart.
- Arteries **(except pulmonary artery)** always carry oxgenated blood. The pulmonary artery is the only artery, which carries deoxygenated blood. The pulmonary artery carries deoxygenated blood from the right ventricle to the lungs.

- Arteries carry blood under high pressure. To prevent bursting, arteries need to be muscular. They have thick muscular walls and a small lumen.
- Arteries branch into capillaries.

Capillaries
- Capillaries are blood vessels, which are one-cell thick. This allows substances such as glucose, oxygen and other nutrients to diffuse from the capillaries into the tissues.
Carbon dioxide and other waste products diffuse from the tissues into the capillaries.
- The pressure inside capillaries is low as they are delicate.
- They branch together to form veins.

Veins
- Veins carry blood to the heart.
- Veins **(except pulmonary vein)** always carry deoxygenated blood.
- Pulmonary vein is the only vein, which carries oxygenated blood. The pulmonary vein carries oxygenated blood from the lungs to the left atrium.
- Veins carry blood under lower pressure. Therefore, they are less muscular than arteries. They have thinner walls but have a larger lumen than arteries

Biology - Blood Circulation

Humans have a double circulatory system. This means that blood passes throughout the heart twice in each cycle. Let us start from the right atrium:
- The right atrium is filled with deoxygenated blood that comes from the superior and inferior vena cava.

- Deoxygenated blood from the right atrium then enters the right ventricle via the tricuspid valve. When the right ventricle is filled, the tricuspid valve closes to prevent backflow of blood.

- The high pressure inside the right ventricle causes the pulmonary valve to open. The muscles of the right ventricle push the deoxygenated blood into the pulmonary artery. The pulmonary valve closes to prevent backflow of blood.

- The pulmonary artery carries the deoxygenated blood to the lungs. There, gas exchange occurs at the alveoli. The blood becomes oxygenated.

- The pulmonary vein carries the oxygenated blood from the lungs to the left atrium of the heart.

- The oxygenated blood then goes to the left ventricle via the mitral valve. When the left ventricle is filled, the mitral valve closes to prevent backflow of blood.

- The high pressure inside the left ventricle causes the aortic valve to open. The muscles of the left ventricle push the oxygenated blood into the aorta. The aortic valve closes to prevent backflow of blood.

- The aorta then carries the oxygenated blood to the rest of the body.

- Gas exchange occurs in the body tissues and the blood again becomes deoxygenated.

- The inferior and superior vena cava carry deoxygenated blood from the body tissues to the right atrium and the whole process happens again.

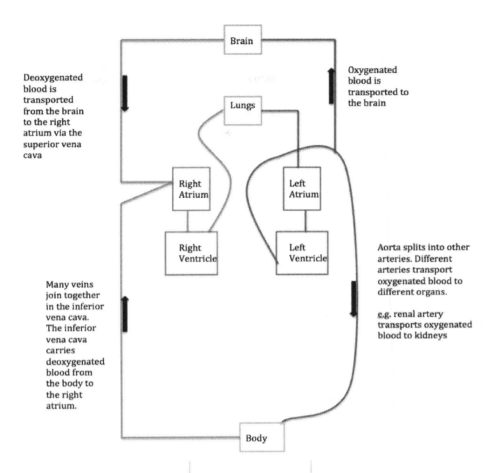

Deoxygenated blood is transported from the brain to the right atrium via the superior vena cava

Oxygenated blood is transported to the brain

Many veins join together in the inferior vena cava. The inferior vena cava carries deoxygenated blood from the body to the right atrium.

Aorta splits into other arteries. Different arteries transport oxygenated blood to different organs.

e.g. renal artery transports oxygenated blood to kidneys

Why is the left ventricle more muscular than the right ventricle? The left ventricle needs to be more muscular than the right ventricle.

This is because the right ventricle only needs to push the blood to the lungs, which is a short distance. However, the left ventricle needs to push blood to the rest of the body, which is a much greater distance. It needs more force to do so, and hence, is more muscular than the right ventricle.

Biology - Initiation of Heartbeat

The atria and ventricles contract and relax alternatively to pump blood through your heart.
Our heartbeat is initiated by electrical impulses that travel down a pathway in our heart.

1) Sinoatrial node (SAN)
This is the heart's natural pacemaker. The SAN is located in the **right atrium**. It contains a small bundle of specialised cells, which start the impulse. The electrical activity spreads through the walls of the atria, which causes them to contract.
This causes the blood to travel from the atria to ventricles.

2) Atrioventricular node (AVN)
The AVN is a group of cells in the centre of the heart. It acts as an insulating layer between the atria and ventricles. It slows down the electrical signal before the signal enters the ventricles. This allows the ventricles to contract **after** the atria have finished contracting.
3) Bundle of His and Purkinje Fibres
These fibres provide a pathway to send the impulse to the muscular walls of the ventricles and cause them to

contract. The right ventricle sends the blood to the lungs and the left ventricle sends the blood to the body.

4) The Cycle Repeats
The SAN initiates another impulse and the cycle repeats.
The atria and ventricles contract and relax alternatively to pump blood through your heart.
Our heartbeat is initiated by electrical impulses that travel down a pathway in our heart.

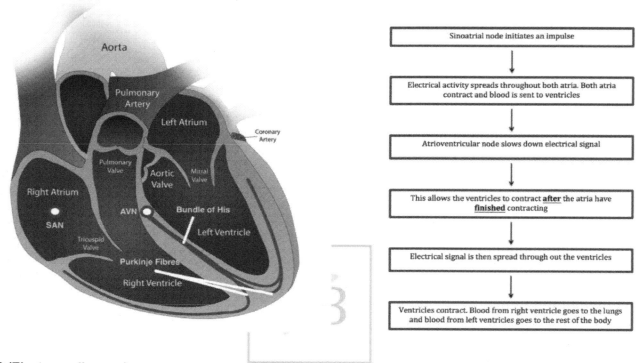

Sinoatrial node initiates an impulse

↓

Electrical activity spreads throughout both atria. Both atria contract and blood is sent to ventricles

↓

Atrioventricular node slows down electrical signal

↓

This allows the ventricles to contract **after** the atria have **finished** contracting

↓

Electrical signal is then spread through out the ventricles

↓

Ventricles contract. Blood from right ventricle goes to the lungs and blood from left ventricles goes to the rest of the body

ECG (Electrocardiogram)
An electrocardiogram is a test to check a person's heart's rhythm and electrical activity.
Sensors are attached to the skin to detect electrical signals produced by the heart each time it beats.
An ECG is used to diagnose and monitor heart conditions such as heart attacks and coronary heart disease.

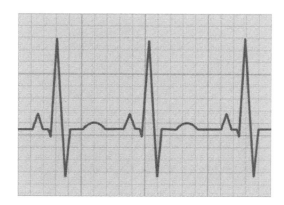

Biology - Digestive System

Digestion is the breakdown of food into smaller components until they can be absorbed and assimilated into the body.
The parts of our body that are involved in the process of digestion, together, make up the digestive system.

Mouth

Digestion starts as soon as food enters your mouth. The saliva contains an enzyme called **amylase**, which breaks **starch into sugar**.

Mechanical digestion also occurs in the mouth. The action of teeth breaking a large piece of food into smaller bits aids amylase action. By breaking large pieces of food into smaller ones, we increase the total surface area of the food pieces. Therefore, the amylase is able to efficiently break starch into sugars.

The small pieces of food that we swallow are called a **bolus**.
The food then enters the **oesophagus**. The oesophagus is a muscular tube and its function is to transport food and liquid from the mouth to the stomach.

No absorption takes place in the oesophagus.

Stomach

The stomach is a sac-like organ, which is made up of strong muscular walls. It holds the food for some time. - The food is churned and mixed in the stomach.
The stomach also secretes hydrochloric acid (HCl) and an inactivated enzyme called pepsinogen.

Function of HCl:
HCl is an acid, which plays an important role in the immune system. It kills any harmful bacteria and parasites, which are ingested with the food.
It also activates pepsinogen into pepsin.

Function of Pepsinogen
Pepsinogen is activated by the HCl into pepsin. Pepsin is a protease enzyme, which breaks large protein molecules into amino acids.

Pancreas

The pancreas secretes lipase, carbohydrase and protease enzymes into the small intestine. They continue the digestion process.

Small Intestine

In the small intestine, bile from the gall bladder and enzymes from the pancreas come to continue the digestion of food.
- Bile contains bile acids, which are critical for digestion and absorption of fats and fat-soluble vitamins.
- The digested molecules of food are then absorbed by the villi present in the small intestine.
- Villi are finger-like projections, which increase the surface area for the absorption of digested food.
- The food then enters the large intestine.

Large Intestine

Faeces or food waste from the digestive process travels across the large intestine by contractions of the tube.
Faeces is then stored in the last part of the large intestine, which is the rectum.
The faeces is stored by closing the muscular sphincters.

Anus

The brain decides whether the rectal contents can be released or not. If they can, the sphincters relax and the rectum contracts, expelling its contents.
Food is egested from the body via the anus.

Enzyme	Action	Location
Carbohydrase	Starch to Sugars	Salivary Glands
Protease	Proteins to Amino Acids	Stomach, Pancreas
Lipase	Fats to Fatty Acids	Pancreas

Biology - Enzymes

Enzymes are **biological catalysts**. A catalyst is a substance or chemical that increases the rate of reaction without being used up. A biological catalyst is catalytic system that exists in living systems. Therefore, enzymes are biological catalysts, which speed up reactions inside our bodies without being used up.

Each enzyme is **specific** to its substrate. The enzymes break down substrates and the molecules that form after these catalytic reactions are called **products**.

The **active site** of an enzyme is the region where the substrate attaches. The shape of the active site is **complementary** to the shape of the substrate.

When enzymes and substrates collide, they form an **enzyme -substrate complex**. The reaction takes place within this complex and the products are then released. After the reaction, the enzyme can catalyse another substrate.

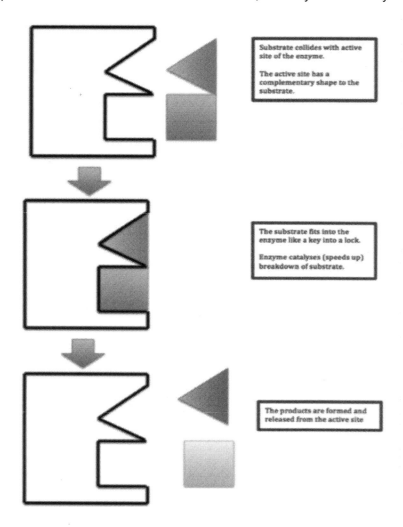

Substrate collides with active site of the enzyme.

The active site has a complementary shape to the substrate.

The substrate fits into the enzyme like a key into a lock.

Enzyme catalyses (speeds up) breakdown of substrate.

The products are formed and released from the active site

Effect of Temperature on Enzyme Activity

As temperature increases to the optimum temperature, the kinetic energies of the enzyme and substrate increase. This increases the number of collisions between the enzyme and substrate. This allows more enzyme-substrate complexes to form, leading to an increase in enzyme activity.

If temperature increases beyond the optimum, the enzyme becomes denatured. Its active site changes shape so that no substrates can attach to it. So no enzyme-substrate complexes form. This decreases the rate of enzyme activity substantially.

NOTE: Denaturation is a **permanent** change.

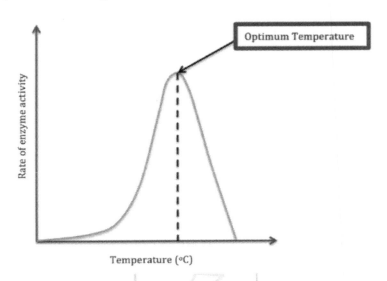

Effect of pH on Enzyme Activity

Every enzyme has its own optimum pH. If the pH deviates from this optimum (i.e. becomes too low or too high), the enzyme's active site denatures. It loses its complementary shape, which prevents the formation of enzyme-substrate complexes. This decreases enzyme activity.

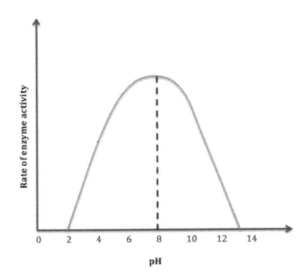

Digestive enzymes

Digestive enzymes are involved in the breakdown of food in our body.

Proteases

Proteases break down proteins into amino acids.

Region in body	Name of protease	Region of production	Substrate	Product
Stomach	Pepsin	Glands in stomach	Proteins	Amino acids
Duodenum	Trypsin	Pancreas	Proteins	Amino acids
Ileum	Peptidase	Wall of ileum	Proteins	Amino acids

Carbohydrases

Carbohydrases break down carbohydrates into sugars.

Region in body	Name of protease	Region of production	Substrate	Product
Mouth	Salivary amylase	Salivary glands	Starch	Maltose
Duodenum	Pancreatic amylase	Pancreas	Starch	Maltose
Ileum	Amylase	Wall of ileum	Maltose	Glucose

Lipases

Lipases break down lipids into fatty acids and glycerol.

Region in body	Name of protease	Region of production	Substrate	Product
Duodenum	Lipase	Pancreas	Lipids	Fatty acids and glycerol

Biology - Kidneys and Nephrons

Kidneys are organs, which are located in the back of the abdomen. They have two primary functions:
1) Regulation of water content in blood
2) Removal of toxic, metabolic waste from the body

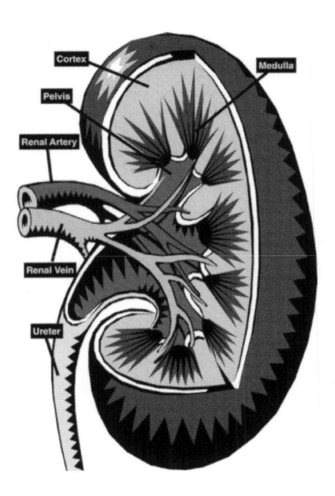

The Process

1) Oxygenated blood is brought to the kidney via the **renal artery**.

2) The kidney controls water and salt contents and removes waste products such as excess water and urea.

3) The filtered, waste products form a liquid called **urine**.

4) The urine is then transported to the **bladder** by ureters for **storage**.

5) When the bladder fills up, nerve signals are sent to the brain. When it is convenient, the urine is then expelled from the body through the urethra.

6) The purified, deoxygenated blood returns to the circulation via the **renal vein**.
The kidneys also contain **nephrons**. These structures are responsible for regulating water and salt levels and removing urea from the blood

Nephrons

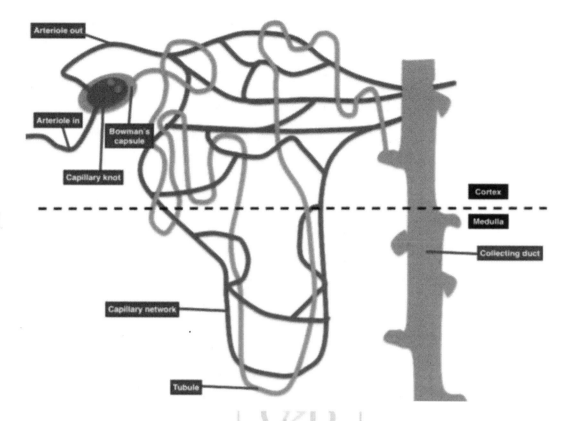

The nephrons consist of the **Bowman's capsule**, which surrounds a **capillary knot** (**Glomerulus**) . In the glomerulus, high pressure is produced. The arteriole going into the glomerulus is wider than the capillary going out. This change in diameter causes high pressure to be created.

This pressure results in **ultrafiltration**. In ultrafiltration, the glomerulus filters water, ions, glucose and other small molecules from the blood.

Some large molecules such as proteins and red blood cells are too big to leave the capillary and enter the tubule.

Selective reabsorption occurs in the rest of the tubule. In this, glucose, some salts and water are reabsorbed into the blood.

The **collecting duct** is responsible for reabsorbing water and sending urine to the ureter.

Role of Kidneys in Homeostasis
You can learn more about the role of kidneys in homeostasis in the 'Homeostasis' topic.

Biology - Homeostasis

Homeostasis basically means the state of balance in internal conditions maintained by living organisms.
Living cells need their environment to be ideal for them in order to survive.
The nervous system and hormones are responsible for this.

Here are some things that need to be in balance in living things:

- Temperature
- Blood glucose
- Water content

Temperature
The hypothalamus is the part of the brain, which monitors body temperature. It receives information from temperature-sensitive receptors present in the skin and circulatory system.

When it is too hot, we want to maximise heat loss from our body:

- Sweat glands release more sweat. Sweat evaporates, creating a 'cooling effect'.
- Blood vessels dilate (become wider), allowing more blood to flow and more heat to be lost.
- The hair on the skin become flat, trapping less air, preventing insulation

When it is too cold, we want to minimise heat loss from our body:

- Blood vessels constrict (become narrower), allowing less blood to flow and less heat to be lost.
- The hair on the skin rise, trapping more air, creating some insulation and preventing heat loss
- Shivering occurs, causing rapid muscle contractions, releasing heat.

Blood Glucose
Insulin is the main hormone, which helps to control blood glucose concentration. It is produced by the pancreas.
Insulin causes the liver to convert glucose to glycogen. Glycogen is primarily stored in the liver.

When blood glucose is low, insulin is not secreted into the blood. Hence, glucose is not converted into glycogen. Therefore, blood glucose concentration increases.

When blood glucose is high, insulin is secreted into the blood. Hence, glucose is converted into glycogen. Therefore, blood glucose concentration decreases.

Water Content
How do we lose water?

- Sweat
- Urine
- Faeces

It is important to keep constant water content in the body, as our cells require water in order to function efficiently.

A hormone that plays a crucial role in maintaining body water content is the **anti-diuretic hormone (ADH)**.

- When the blood water content is low, the hypothalamus sends a signal to the pituitary gland. The pituitary gland releases more ADH into the bloodstream and it travels to the kidneys. ADH causes the kidneys to reabsorb more water back into the body.
  This produces more concentrated (yellowish) urine.

- When the blood water content is high, the hypothalamus sends a signal to the pituitary gland. The pituitary gland releases less ADH into the bloodstream.
  This causes the kidneys to reabsorb less water back into the body. More water leaves the body. This produces more dilute (clear) urine.

Biology - Hormones

Hormones	Function	Site of Secretion
Insulin	Maintains blood sugar level	Pancreas
Glucagon	Increases blood sugar level	Pancreas
ADH	Regulates amount of water in blood	Pituitary Gland
Adrenaline	Increases heart rate, blood pressure	Adrenal Glands (kidney)
Testosterone	Mainly sperm production	Testes
Oestrogen (female)	Stimulates the growth of uterus lining	Ovaries
Progesterone (female)	Maintains the uterus lining	Ovaries
Oxytocin (female)	Releases breast milk	Posterior pituitary
Prolactin (female)	Milk production in mammary glands	Anterior pituitary

Biology - Meiosis

Meiosis is the cell division process for the production of gametes. Gametes are sex cells: sperm in males and eggs in females.

Meiosis results in the production of four daughter cells with exactly **half as many chromosomes** as the parent cell. The daughter cells are **haploid**, as they have half as many chromosomes.
The parent cell is **diploid** since it has double the number of chromosomes as the daughter cells.

When an egg cell and a sperm cell, which are both haploid, combine during fertilisation, they make a zygote, which is diploid.
Haploid + Haploid = Diploid

Unlike mitosis, meiosis is a **two-step** division process: Meiosis I and Meiosis II.

Homologous chromosomes form homologous chromosome pairs with each coming from each parent. They are similar in length, gene position and centromere location.

In the first step of the division process (Meiosis I), the homologous pairs are separated.
In the second step (Meiosis II), the sister chromatids are separated.

Stages of Meiosis I:
- Prophase I
- Metaphase I
- Anaphase I
- Telophase I

Stages of Meiosis II:
- Prophase II
- Metaphase II
- Anaphase II
- Telophase II

Meiosis I

- **Interphase**
  Interphase is the phase of the cell cycle in which the cell copies its DNA in preparation for the cell division.
  The cell organelles double in number, the DNA replicates and protein synthesis occurs. The chromosomes are not visible and the DNA appears as uncoiled chromatin.

- **Prophase I**
  During prophase I, chromosomes begin to condense.
  Homologous pairs also form. The two match up at corresponding positions according to their length.
  Crossing-over occurs in this stage of meiosis. This means that fragments of DNA from each chromosome are exchanged between each other in the homologous pair. Crossing-over leads to variation in individuals of the same species.

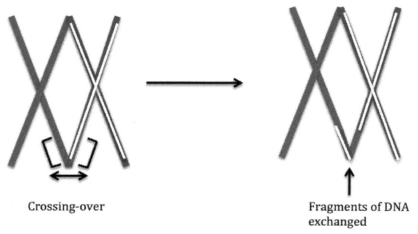

Crossing-over   Fragments of DNA
                                 exchanged

Crossing-over of DNA fragments

After crossing over, the spindle begins to capture chromosomes.
Unlike mitosis, each chromosome from the homologous pair attaches to the microtubule from the opposite pole.

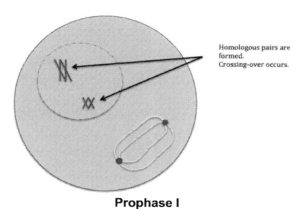

Homologous pairs are
formed.
Crossing-over occurs.

Prophase I

- **Metaphase I**
  Homologous pairs line up at the equator.
  The pairs' assortment at the equator is random. Their lineup at the equator is completely not fixed. This, like crossing-over, leads to variation in individuals of the same species. This is known as **random assortment**.

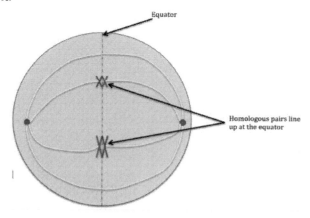

Equator

Homologous pairs line
up at the equator

Metaphase I

- **Anaphase I**
  The homologues are pulled towards opposite poles. The **sister chromatids** however, remain attached to each other.

- **Telophase I**
  The chromosomes arrive at the opposite poles.
  The chromosomes decondense and the nuclear membrane reforms.

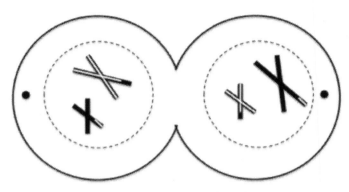

Each chromosome has two (non-identical) sister chromatids

Telophase I

- **Cytokinesis**
  The cytoplasm of the parent cell divides, forming two haploid daughter cells.

Meiosis II

No copying of DNA occurs in meiosis II. The cells that enter meiosis II are the ones that completed meiosis I. They are haploid but their chromosomes still consist of two sister chromatids.
The main purpose of meiosis II is to separate these two sister chromatids.

- **Prophase II**
  During prophase II, chromosomes begin to condense.
  The spindle forms and the microtubules begin to attach to chromosomes. The two sister chromatids of each chromosome attach to opposite spindles.

- **Metaphase II**
  The chromosomes line up individually along the equator.

- **Anaphase II**
  The **sister chromatids** separate and are pulled towards the opposite poles.

- **Telophase II**
  The chromosomes decondense and the nuclear membrane reforms.

- **Cytokinesis**
  In meiosis I, two haploid daughter cells are formed.
  In meiosis II, the two haploid daughter cells, each, form two more haploid daughter cells.
  Therefore, in total, (2 x 2) 4 haploid daughter cells are produced.

Biology - Mitosis

Mitosis is a type of cell division in which one parent cell divides into two genetically identical daughter cells.

The daughter cells produced are **diploid**. Diploid is a term given to cells which have two sets of chromosomes.

Mitosis is the cell division, which occurs for all our body cell **except gametes**. Gametes are produced by **meiosis**.

Phases of Mitosis

- Prophase

- Metaphase

- Anaphase

- Telophase

Interphase occurs before the actual process of mitosis.

- **Interphase**
  Interphase is the phase of the cell cycle in which the cell copies its DNA in preparation for the cell division.
  The cell organelles double in number, the DNA replicates and protein synthesis occurs. The chromosomes are not visible and the DNA appears as uncoiled chromatin.

- **Prophase**
  During prophase, chromosomes begin to condense.
  The spindle forms and the microtubules begin to attach to chromosomes. The two sister chromatids of each chromosome attach to opposite spindles.

- **Metaphase**
  The chromosomes line up individually along the equator.

- **Anaphase**
  The **sister chromatids** separate and are pulled towards the opposite poles.

- **Telophase**
  The spindle breaks down.
  The chromosomes decondense and the nuclear membrane reforms.

- **Cytokinesis**
  This is the division of the cytoplasm to form two new cells. In animals, cytokinesis is contractile.

When cytokinesis finishes, we end up with two new cells, each with a complete set of chromosomes. These cells are identical to the parent cell.

Biology - Natural Selection

Natural selection is a process in which organisms who are better adapted to their environment tend to have better chances of survival and produce more offsprings.

Organisms with advantageous alleles are better adapted to their environment. These organisms then reproduce and pass on these advantageous alleles to their offspring. This eventually leads to evolution.

Natural selection helps us to understand evolution better and gives us an idea of why organisms are of different shapes and sizes.

Example:
Let us say that in a park, there are green worms and red worms.
The green worms can camouflage in the green grass but the red worms will stand out. The predators will then eat the red ones as they are easier to spot.
The green worms will survive because they have the advantageous allele, which gives them their green colour.
They will reproduce and pass these advantageous alleles to their offspring.

In the example above, the green colour and the red colour of the worms are their phenotypes.
A phenotype is a visible characteristic of an organism, which comes about as a result of their genes.

Natural Selection was first expounded by Charles Darwin.

The Process:

1) Mutation
Differences in DNA in individuals of the same species arise.

2) Variation
Physical differences in individuals of the same species arise.
e.g. some worms are green and some are red

3) Competitive Advantage
Some individuals become more adapted to their environment. They outcompete others for resources.

4) Survival of the Fittest
Those that are better adapted to their environment have better chances of survival.
e.g. green worms are more likely to survive in a park than red worms

5) Reproduction
Those that are better suited to their environment have more offspring.

6) Passing advantageous alleles
Those that are better adapted to their environment are able to pass on their advantageous alleles to their offspring. Therefore, their offspring are also better suited for their environment.

Biology - Central Nervous System

Our central nervous system is made up of the **brain** and the **spinal cord**.

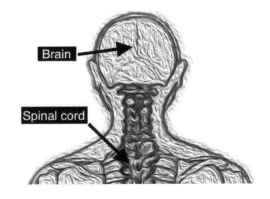

Nerve cells, also known as **neurons**, carry electrical impulses around the body.

Structure of A Neurone

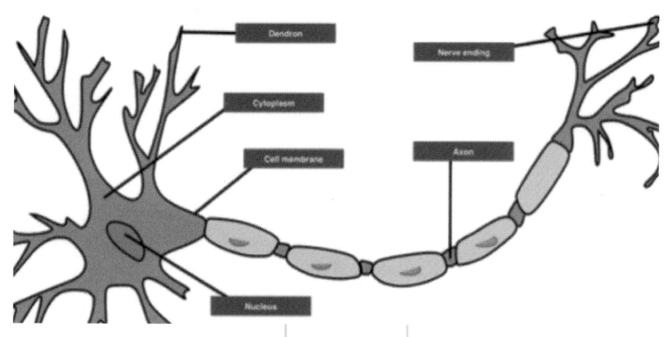

The **axons** carry messages up and down the cell body.
The **dendrons** branch into **dendrites** at each end and these receive **impulses** from other neurones.

Types of Neurons

There are three types of neurons:

1) Sensory neurons
2) Relay neurons
3) Motor neurons

• Sensory neurons are activated when they receive some sensory input from our surrounding. As the name suggests, when we 'sense' something.
• E.g. touching a hot object.
• The sensory neurons then send signals to the rest of the nervous system.
• Relay neurones connect sensory neurons to motor neurons.
• Motor neurons connect to muscles, glands and organs throughout the body. They control all of our muscle movements.

The roles of these three types of neurons in the reflex arc are discussed in the topic 'Reflex Arc'.

Synapses

Synapses are small gaps between two neurons.

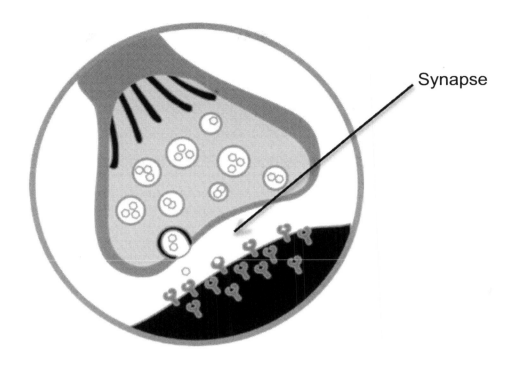

Synapse

Effects of Drugs on Synapses

1) **Stimulants** (which increase alertness) cause more neurotransmitter molecules to diffuse across the synapse.

2) **Depressants** (slow down CNS) stop the next neuron from sending nerve impulses. They slow down signals in the nerves and brain.

Biology - Reflex Arc

A reflex action is an automatic and rapid response to a stimulus, which minimises any potential damage to the body.

It is essential for survival of organisms.
Reflex actions are therefore RAP:
- **R**apid
- **A**utomatic
- **P**rotective

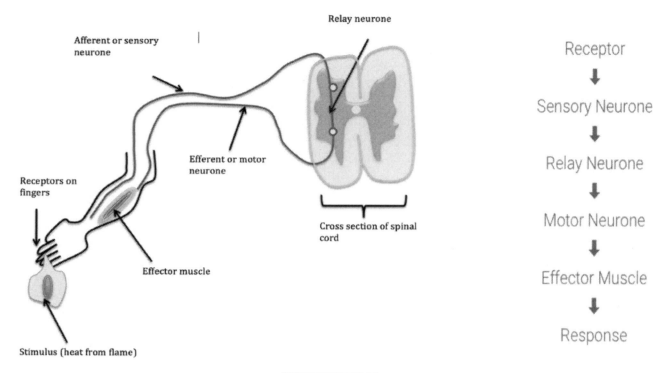

The Pathway:
Let us use the example of someone touching something very hot.

1) Receptors in the skin detect a stimulus (something hot i.e. change in temperature)
2) The receptors send an electrical signal along the sensory neurone
3) The sensory neurone then sends these electrical impulses to a relay neurone in the spinal cord
4) The relay neurone connects the sensory neurone to a motor neurone
5) The electrical impulses then travel along the motor neurone towards the an effector muscle
6) The effector muscle produces a movement, which is rapid, automatic and protective
7) In this case, the effector muscle moves the hand away from the hot object

---

Biology - Asexual and Sexual Reproduction

Asexual Reproduction

In asexual reproduction, only one parent is required. It does NOT involve sex cells or fertilisation.

Since there is only **one parent** , the offspring are **genetically identical** to the parent and each other. We call these **clones** since there is no mixing of genetic information.

E.g. Bacteria reproduce asexually

Sexual Reproduction

In sexual reproduction, two parents are involved. This causes genetic information from both parents to mix and produce offspring that resemble both parents but **NOT identical** to them.

Sexual reproduction involved sex cells (gametes) and fertilisation. The fusion of a male gamete and female gamete is called fertilisation.

Sexual reproduction leads to increased variation since offspring are genetically different.

Biology - Inheritance

Inheritance refers to the passing of genes and alleles from parents to offspring. Different combinations of these genes and alleles give each individual their unique personality and characteristics.

Some Inheritance Key Terms

Key Term	Meaning	Example
Genes	Small section of DNA on a chromosome, which does for a particular sequence of amino acids to make a certain protein.	Gene for Eye colour
Alleles	Different versions of the same gene	Allele for brown coloured eyes is 'B'. Allele for blue coloured eyes is 'b'.
Dominant allele	The allele, which is always expressed, even if only one copy is present. They are represented by a capital letter.	In humans, the allele for brown eyes (B) is dominant and allele for blue eyes (b) is recessive. So if a person is heterozygous (Bb), their eye colour would be brown.
Recessive allele	A recessive allele is not expressed if a dominant allele is present. A recessive allele is only expressed when there are two copies of it, i.e. the organism is homozygous recessive. Recessive alleles are represented by a lower case letter.	In humans, the allele for brown eyes (B) is dominant and allele for blue eyes (b) is recessive. So if a person is heterozygous (Bb), their eye colour would be brown. However, if the person was homozygous recessive, i.e., 'bb', they would have blue coloured eyes.
Heterozygous	Alleles are both different for the same characteristic. In this case, the dominant allele is expressed. However, they would also be a 'carrier' of the recessive allele.	Inheriting brown-eye gene from one parent and blue-eye gene from other parent. Their genotype would be 'Bb'. In this case the person's eye colour would be brown because allele for brown colour (B) is dominant over allele for blue colour (b).
Homozygous	Both alleles are identical for the same characteristics.	If a person inherits brown eye genes from **both** parents, their genotype would be 'BB'. They are hence called homozygous dominant. If a person inherits blue eye genes from **both** parents, their genotype would be 'bb'. They are hence called homozygous recessive.
Phenotype	The visible characteristic of an organism, which occurs as a result of its genes and alleles. Something that is visual from the outside.	The brown colour of someone's eye is a phenotype.
Genotype	The alleles that an organism has for a characteristic	BB, Bb, bb

Monohybrid Crosses

Let us say an organism, which is homozygous recessive for a particular gene, mates with another organism, which is heterozygous for the same gene. To find out what the genotype of the offspring would be, we use a **punnet square**.

Example:
A condition is caused by a recessive allele. If one parent is heterozygous for this gene and the other parent is homozygous recessive, what is the probability that the child will have the condition?

Let us say that the dominant allele is **D** and the recessive allele is **d**. For the child to have the condition, they must be homozygous recessive.

	D	d
d	Dd	dd
d	Dd	dd

As we can see, there is a 50% chance that the child will be homozygous recessive (dd) and have the condition. There is a 50% chance that the child will be heterozygous (Dd) and not have the condition.

We can show this as a ratio too.
Homozygous recessive : Heterozygous = 2 : 2 = 1 : 1

You can be given many combinations in the BMAT exam such as:

1) Heterozygous with homozygous recessive
2) Heterozygous with heterozygous
3) Homozygous recessive with homozygous recessive
4) Homozygous dominant with homozygous dominant
5) Homozygous recessive with heterozygous

Try doing the combinations mentioned above and find out the percentage probability that the child will have the condition.

Family Pedigrees

Since I have completed all past papers, I can safely say family pedigree questions are common in the BMAT exam. It is important for you understand how to analyse family pedigrees.

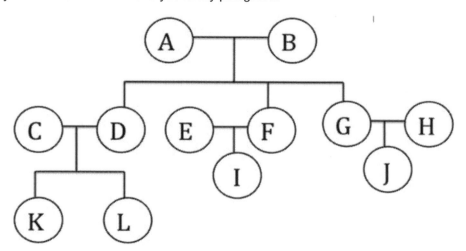

This is what a family pedigree looks like.

From this you can see that, A and B have three children: D, F and G.
E and F have one child: I
D and C have two children: K and L
G and H have one child: J

Example:
In the family pedigree above, A and B are heterozygous for a condition. What is the probability that F is homozygous recessive?

Let us say the dominant allele is **A** and recessive allele is **a**. Since A and B are both heterozygous, we can draw the following punnet square.

	A	a
A	AA	Aa
a	Aa	aa

From the punnet square, you can see that there is 25% chance that F is homozygous recessive.

Trickier Example:
Huntington's disease is an inherited condition. It is caused by the dominant allele.

A is homozygous dominant whilst B is homozygous recessive. If C is heterozygous, what is the percentage probability that K has the Huntington's disease?

Try solving this problem on your own first and then check the solution.

Solution:
Let the dominant allele be **H** and recessive allele be **h**.

In order to have Huntington's disease, you need to have either of the following genotypes: HH or Hh Draw

a punnet square for the cross between A and B.

	H	H
h	Hh	Hh
h	Hh	Hh

As you can see that there is a 100% probability that D is heterozygous. We know that C is heterozygous too. We now draw a punnet square for the cross between C and D.

	H	h
H	HH	Hh
h	Hh	hh

In order to have Huntington's disease, you need to have either of the following genotypes: HH or Hh So percentage probability that K has the condition = 75%

Biology - DNA and Protein Synthesis

DNA (Deoxyribonucleic acid)

DNA is the hereditary material in all humans and nearly all organisms. DNA is found in the **nucleus** of our cells, in the form of **chromosomes**. Nearly every cell in a person's body has the same DNA.

Structure of DNA

DNA is made up of **nucleotides**.
A nucleotide is a molecule, which contains a phosphate group, one sugar group and one nitrogen base.

In DNA, the nucleotides have the sugar group **deoxyribose**. There are four nitrogenous bases: adenine (A), Guanine (G), Thymine (T) and Cytosine (C). The **order of these bases** determines DNA's instructions or genetic code.

NOTE: Adenine always bonds with Thymine and Cytosine always bonds with Guanine. AT and CG are **complementary base pairs**.

In DNA, nucleotides are attached together to from two long strands that spiral to create a structure called the double helix.

The sugar phosphates form the 'backbone' of the DNA molecule, whilst the complementary base pairs are in the middle. The bases of one strand pair up with their complementary bases on the other strand.

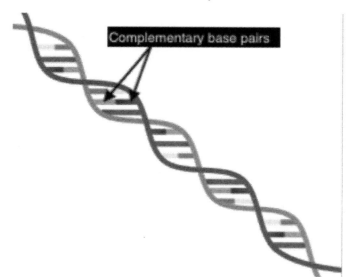

DNA molecules are very long. In order to fit DNA in our cells, they need to be coiled tightly to form **chromosomes**.

Protein Synthesis

Protein synthesis involves the production of It is important for you to understand that genes carry the code for proteins. **Triplets** of bases in DNA code for amino acids. The order of amino acids in a protein is determined by the order of base triplets in DNA.

The first step in protein synthesis is **transcription**. In the nucleus, enzymes transcribe a molecule of mRNA. The sequence of bases in mRNA is complementary to the sequence of bases on the DNA.

The second step in protein synthesis is **translation**. After DNA is transcribed into mRNA, the mRNA work together with tRNA and ribosomes to produce a protein.

Gene Mutations

When a cell divides, the DNA replicates carefully to preserve the genetic information. However, changes in DNA can occur. This change in the DNA is a gene mutation.

Some mutations can affect a few bases whilst others can affect one or more chromosomes.

Biology - Gene Modification and Stem Cells

Genetic Modification

In genetic modification, a gene from one species is taken and is put into another species.

Method:
1) The desired characteristic is **selected**
2) The gene responsible for the desired characteristic is then **isolated**
3) The gene is then **inserted** into another organism

Examples of genetic modification:
1) Cloning – produces a genetically identical copy of an organism
2) Pesticide – resistant crops

Stem Cells

Stem cells are cells found in the early stages of development of an embryo. These cells have not **differentiated**.
In differentiation, an unspecialised cell becomes a more specialised cell type. So stem cells are unspecialised cells.

If these cells are removed from the embryo, they will differentiate into any type of cell.
So **embryonic** stem cells can give rise to any cell type.

However, as an animal matures, the cells lose this ability. **Adult** stem cells can only differentiate into related cell types. For example, bone marrow cells can differentiate into blood cells and immune system cells but not other types of cells.

Biology - Sex Determination

In most mammals, females are XX whilst males are XY.

This means that in females, the sex chromosomes are **homozygous** – two X chromosomes. Therefore, all eggs (female gametes) have chromosome X.

In males, sex chromosomes are **heterozygous** – one X and one Y chromosome. Therefore, 50% of a male's sperm has the X chromosome and the other 50% have the Y chromosome.

During fertilisation, there is a 50% probability that an X chromosome–containing sperm fertilizes the egg and 50% probability that a Y chromosome–containing sperm fertilizes the egg.

This means that there is an equal probability that the offspring will be male or female. We can show this using a Punnet Square.

	X	Y
X	XX	XY
X	XX	XY

This punnet square shows that there is a 50% probability that the offspring will be a girl and a 50% probability that the offspring will be a boy.

Biology - Carbon and Nitrogen Cycles

Carbon Cycle

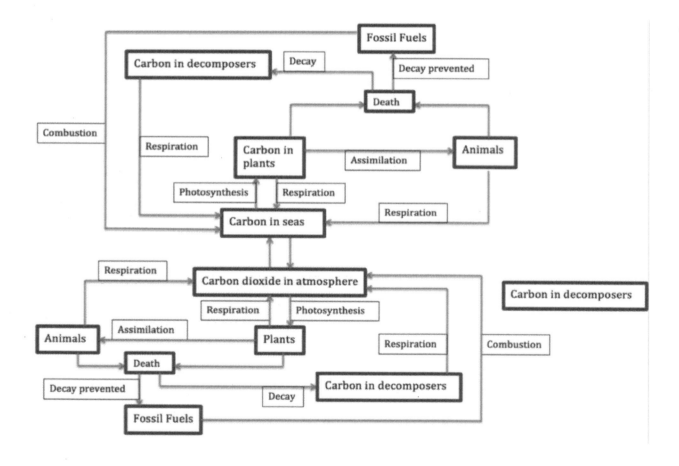

Nitrogen Cycle

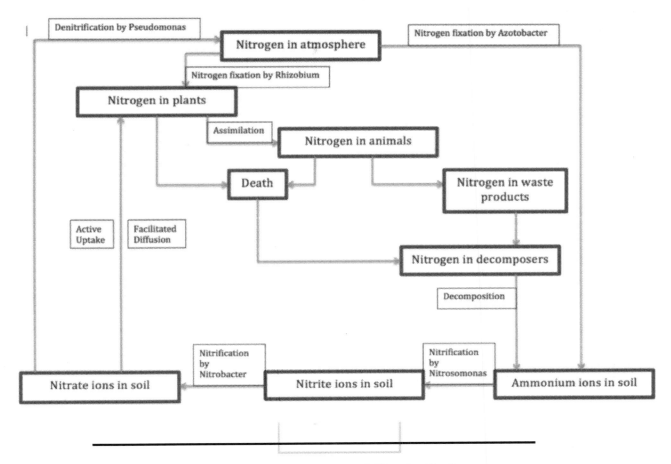

Biology - Disease and Body Defence

Some microorganisms, which enter our body can cause diseases and harm us. Such disease-causing microorganisms are called **pathogens**.

In order to fight these pathogens, our body has an immune system. Our immune system consists of two types of white blood cells (**phagocytes** and **lymphocytes**).

Phagocytes
Phagocytes engulf pathogens. The phagocytes' membranes surround the pathogen and enzymes inside the cell break down the pathogen and destroy it.

Lymphocytes
Lymphocytes recognise proteins on the surface of the pathogen. These proteins are called **antigens**. Lymphocytes identify these antigens as 'foreign' and produce **antibodies** since those antigens are not naturally occurring with the body.

An antibody is a protein produced by the immune system to attack any foreign organisms that enter our body.

If some pathogens produce toxins, lymphocytes can also produce **antitoxins** to neutralise those toxins.

Note:
Phagocytes are ' **non-specific'** since they engulf all pathogens they encounter. On the other hand, lymphocytes are **'specific'** since the antibodies and antitoxins that they produce are highly specific to the antigen on the pathogen.

Biology - Food Chains and Organism Interactions

Organism	Definition
Producer	An organism, which makes its own organic nutrients.
Consumer	An organism, which feeds on other organisms.
Primary consumer	An organism, which feeds on the producer. A primary consumer is usually a herbivore.
Secondary consumer	An organism, which feeds on primary consumers.
Tertiary consumer	An organism, which feeds on secondary consumers.
Herbivore	An organism, which feeds on plants only.
Carnivore	An organism, which feeds on animals only.
Omnivore	An organism, which feeds on both plants and animals.
Decomposer	An organism, which feeds on the dead and decaying organisms. They also feed on the faeces of animals.

A food chain shows the feeding relationship between organisms. In simpler words, it shows what eats what.

A food chain always begins with a **producer**. A producer is an organism, which produces its own organ nutrients. This is usually a green plant that obtains energy from the **Sun** by **photosynthesis**. The sun is the ultimate source of energy.

The other organisms in the food chain are **consumers**. A consumer is an organism, which feeds on other organisms.

A **food web** is a series of interlinked food webs.

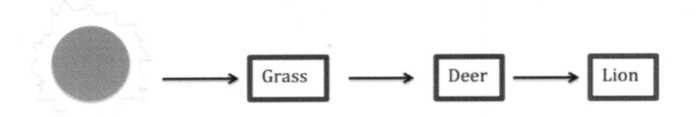

Energy Transfer in Food Chains

Energy is transferred in the form of energy-rich molecules when one organism eats another organism.
However, this transfer of energy is inefficient.
Approximately, only **10% of the energy** is transferred from one organism to another.
This inefficient energy flow limits the length of the food chain.

Pyramid of Biomass

A pyramid of biomass shows the total mass of organisms at each trophic level.
Biomass refers to the dry mass of an organism.

It must be noted that not all biomass is passed from one organism to another. About only 10% of the biomass is transferred from each trophic level to the next.
The **tropic level** refers to the position of an organism in a food chain, web or pyramid.

Biomass is lost in the form of excretion, respiration and egestion. Since only 10% is transferred at each trophic level, the total amount of biomass transferred becomes very small after only a few trophic levels. Food chains are therefore limited to 5 or 6 trophic levels.

Symbiotic Relationships

There are various types of interactions between organisms.
We only need to go through 3 of them in this section.

1) Mutualism

Mutualism is a symbiotic interaction between two organisms in which both organisms benefit.
E.g. Egyptian plover and crocodile. The crocodile lies with its mouth open to allow the plover to fly into its mouth and feed on bits of decaying meat stuck in the crocodile's teeth. The crocodile gets its teeth cleaned whilst the plover gets the food.

2) Commensalism

Commensalism is a symbiotic interaction between two organisms in which one organism benefits whilst the other is unaffected.
E.g. a tree and a frog. The frog gets shelter under the tree whilst the tree is unaffected.

3) Parasitism

Parasitism is a symbiotic interaction between two organisms in which one organism (the parasite) benefits whilst the other is harmed.
E.g. tapeworm and human. The tapeworm lives in the human's gut and absorbs the human's nutrients whilst the human suffers from pain and weight loss.

Example of Pyramid of Energy

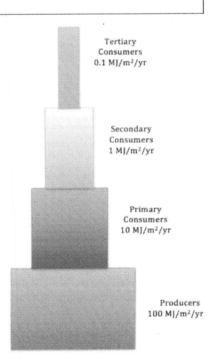

Tertiary Consumers
0.1 MJ/m²/yr

Secondary Consumers
1 MJ/m²/yr

Primary Consumers
10 MJ/m²/yr

Producers
100 MJ/m²/yr

Chemistry - Acids

Acids produce H^+ ions in aqueous solution.

$HCl \rightarrow H^+ + Cl^-$

Acid solutions have pH values less than 7. The lower the pH, the stronger the acid.

Strong Acids

A strong acid is one, which can completely dissociate its H+ ions in water. This means that it can give off the greatest number of hydrogen ions when placed in solution.
e.g. HCl, H_2SO_4

Weak Acids

A weak acid is one, which does not completely dissociate its H+ ions in water. This means that it does not give off many hydrogen ions when placed in solution.
e.g. ethanoic acid, citric acid

Acid Reactions

- **Acid + Metals**
  Acids react with a metal to form a **salt** and **hydrogen gas**. This is a redox reaction.

  Acid + Metal $\rightarrow$ Salt + Hydrogen gas
  E.g. $2HCl + Fe \rightarrow FeCl_2 + H_2$

  Hydrogen's oxidation number in HCl = +I
  Hydrogen's oxidation number in H_2 = 0 Since
  Hydrogen gains electrons, it is reduced.

  Iron's oxidation number in Fe = 0 Iron's
  oxidation number in $FeCl_2$ = +2 Since Iron
  loses electrons, it is oxidised.
  Since reduction and oxidation occurs at the same time, this reaction is a redox reaction.

- **Acid + Metal oxides**
  Acids react with a metal oxide to form a **salt** and **water**.
  Acid + Metal Oxide $\rightarrow$ Salt + Water
  E.g. $2HCl + CaO \rightarrow CaCl_2 + H_2O$

- **Acid + Alkali**
  Acids react with alkali to form a **salt** and **water**.
  Acid + Alkali $\rightarrow$ Salt + Water
  E.g. HCl + NaOH -> NaCl + H_2O
  This is a neutralisation reaction.

- **Acid + Carbonate**
  Acids react with carbonates to form a **salt**, **water** and **carbon dioxide**. Acid
  + Carbonate $\rightarrow$ Salt + Water + Carbon dioxide
  E.g. $2HCl + CaCO_3 \rightarrow CaCl_2 + H_2O + CO_2$

Chemistry - Alkali

Alkalis produce OH^- ions in aqueous solution.

$NaOH \rightarrow Na^+ + OH^-$

Alkaline solutions have pH values more than 7. The higher the pH, the stronger the alkali.

Strong Alkali

A strong alkali is one, which can completely dissociate its OH^- ions in water. This means that it can give off the greatest number of hydroxide ions when placed in solution.
e.g. $NaOH$, $Ca(OH)_2$

Weak Alkali

A weak alkali is one, which does not completely dissociate its OH^- ions in water. This means that it does not give off many hydroxide ions when placed in solution.
e.g. Ammonia (NH_3)

Alkali Reactions

- **Alkali + Acid**
  Acids react with alkali to form a **salt** and **water**.
  Acid + Alkali $\rightarrow$ Salt + Water
  E.g. $HCl + NaOH \rightarrow NaCl + H_2O$
  This is a neutralisation reaction.

Base vs Alkali

Bases are substances, which reach with acids and neutralise them. Many bases are insoluble. The bases, which are soluble, are called alkali. So, an alkali is just a soluble base.

Chemistry - Alkanes

A hydrocarbon is a compound, which only contains carbon and hydrogen atoms as constituent elements.
An alkane is a saturated hydrocarbon. Saturated means that is has **no double bonds** and has the maximum number of hydrogen atoms. All bonds present in an alkane are single bonds.

General formula of alkanes: C_nH_{2n+2}
If (n = 3), the compound would be:
$C_3H_{2(3)+2} = C_3H_8$

Every alkane's name ends in **'-ane'**.
An alkane's prefix always changes according to the number of carbon atoms present in the compound.
Some common alkanes:

Name of Alkane	No. of Carbon Atoms	Formula
Methane	1	CH_4
Ethane	2	C_2H_6
Propane	3	C_3H_8
Butane	4	C_4H_{10}
Pentane	5	C_5H_{12}
Hexane	6	C_6H_{14}
Heptane	7	C_7H_{16}
Octane	8	C_8H_{18}
Nonane	9	C_9H_{20}
Decane	10	$C_{10}H_{22}$

Chemistry - Alkenes

An alkene is an unsaturated hydrocarbon. Unsaturated means that it contains at least **one double bond** and hence does **not** have the maximum number of hydrogen atoms.

The general formula for alkenes: C_nH_{2n}
If (n = 3), the compound would be:
$C_3H_{2(3)} = C_3H_6$

Every alkene's name ends in **'-ene'**.

An alkene's prefix always changes according to the number of carbon atoms present in the compound.

There cannot be an alkene with only 1 carbon atom. There needs to be a minimum of two carbon atoms for there to be a double bond present. So there is no alkene named methene.

Name of Alkene	No. of Carbon Atoms	Formula
Ethene	2	C_2H_4
Propene	3	C_3H_6
Butene	4	C_4H_8
Pentene	5	C_5H_{10}
Hexene	6	C_6H_{12}
Heptene	7	C_7H_{14}
Octene	8	C_8H_{16}
Nonene	9	C_9H_{18}
Decene	10	$C_{10}H_{20}$

Chemistry - Alcohols

Alcohols contain the functional group '**-OH**' in their molecule.

They have the general formula: $C_nH_{2n+1}OH$
If (n = 3), the compound would be:
$C_3H_{2(3)+1}OH = C_3H_7OH$

Every alcohol's name ends in **'-ol'**.

An alcohol's prefix always changes according to the number of carbon atoms present in the compound.

Some common alcohols:

Name of Alcohol	Number of Carbon Atoms	Formula
Methanol	1	CH_3OH
Ethanol	2	C_2H_5OH
Propanol	3	C_3H_7OH
Butanol	4	C_4H_9OH
Pentanol	5	$C_5H_{11}OH$
Hexanol	6	$C_6H_{13}OH$
Heptanol	7	$C_7H_{15}OH$
Octanol	8	$C_8H_{17}OH$
Nonanol	9	$C_9H_{19}OH$
Decanol	10	$C_{10}H_{21}OH$

Chemistry - Carboxylic Acids

Carboxylic acids have the functional group '-**COOH**' in their molecule.

They are also unsaturated as they contain a 'C = O' bond in their molecule.

They have the general formula: $C_nH_{2n+1}COOH$
If (n = 3), the compound would be:
$C_3H_{2(3)+1} = C_3H_7COOH$

Every carboxylic acid's name ends in **'-oic acid'**.

An acid's prefix always changes according to the number of carbon atoms present in the compound.

Some common carboxylic acids:

Name of Alcohol	No. of Carbon Atoms	Formula
Methanoic acid	1	$HCOOH$
Ethanoic acid	2	CH_3COOH
Propanoic acid	3	C_2H_5COOH
Butanoic acid	4	C_3H_7COOH
Pentanoic acid	5	C_4H_9COOH
Hexanoic acid	6	$C_5H_{11}COOH$
Heptanoic acid	7	$C_6H_{13}COOH$
Octanoic acid	8	$C_7H_{15}COOH$
Nonanoic acid	9	$C_8H_{17}COOH$
Decanoic acid	10	$C_9H_{19}COOH$

Chemistry - Balancing Equations

Questions regarding balancing reaction equations are frequent. There is a high chance that you probably came across some whilst doing past papers.

Such question can also be time consuming. However, there is a simpler and more organised way to solve such questions. We can solve such questions using algebraic equations.

We first need to form algebraic equations for each of the elements present in the equation.
We need to compare the number of atoms present on the LHS and RHS for each element.

Let us begin with a simple question.

Example:
$H_2 + aO_2 \rightarrow H_2O$
Find the value of **a**.

Hydrogen
Number of atoms on LHS = 2
Number of atoms on RHS = 2
So Hydrogen is already balanced.

Oxygen
Number of atoms on LHS = a x 2 = 2a
Number of atoms RHS = 1
In order for oxygen atoms to be balanced, we need to satisfy the equation:
2a = 1
Hence, a = ½

The balanced equation would look like:
$$H_2 + \tfrac{1}{2}O_2 \rightarrow H_2O$$

Complicated Question

Try solving this question on your own first using algebraic equations.

$aCa_3(PO_4)_2 + bSiO_2 + cC \rightarrow dCaSiO_3 + eP_4 + fCO$

Calcium
Number of atoms on LHS = 3a
Number of atoms on RHS = d
3a = d —— Equation 1

Phosphorus
Number of atoms on LHS = 2a
Number of atoms on RHS = 4e
2a = 4e
a = 2e —— Equation 2

Oxygen (present in PO₄ and SiO₂)
Number of atoms on LHS = 8a + 2b
Number of atoms on RHS = 3d + f
8a + 2b = 3d + f —— Equation 3

Silicon
Number of atoms on LHS = b
Number of atoms on RHS = d **b**
= d —— Equation 4

Carbon
Number of atoms on LHS = c
Number of atoms on RHS = f **c**
= f —— Equation 5

Let us express everything in terms of 'a'.

We know:
3a = d
Since, b = d,
b = 3a

We know:
a = 2e
$e = {}^a/_2$

Using Equation 4, b =
d 8a + **2d** = 3d + f
8a = d + f

Using Equation 1, 3a = d
8a – f = 3a
8a – 3a = f
f = 5a

Using Equation 4, c = f
c = 5a

So we have the following equations:
b = 3a
d = 3a

f = 5a

c = 5a

e = $\frac{a}{2}$

Assume, a = 1. We would get:

b = 3 (1) = 3

d = 3 (1) = 3

f = 5 (1) = 5

c = 5 (1) = 5

e = ½

We can let it remain like this.

However, if we need to express 'e' as a whole number, we can simply multiply it by 2. However, we would need to multiply all the other variables by 2 too.

a = 2 (1) = 2

b = 2 (3) = 6

c = 2 (5) = 10

d = 2 (3) = 6

e = 2(½) = 1

f = 2(5) = 10

We would get the following equation:

$2Ca_3(PO_4)_2 + 6SiO_2 + 10C \rightarrow 6CaSiO_3 + 1P_4 + 10CO$ We

can check again to see if everything is balanced.

Calcium

Number of atoms on LHS = 6

Number of atoms on RHS = 6

Phosphorus

Number of atoms on LHS = 4

Number of atoms on RHS = 4

Oxygen (present in PO_4 and SiO_2)

Number of atoms on LHS = 16 + 12 = 28

Number of atoms on RHS = 18 + 10 = 28

Silicon

Number of atoms on LHS = 6

Number of atoms on RHS = 6

Carbon

Number of atoms on LHS = 10

Number of atoms on RHS = 10

Chemistry - Types of Reactions

Combination Reaction

In this type of reaction, two or more reactants combine to form a single larger product.

A+B→AB

e.g. $S + O_2 \rightarrow SO_2$

Decomposition Reaction

In this type of reaction, a single reactant is broken down to form two or more products.

AB→A+B

e.g. $CaCO_3 \rightarrow CaO + CO_2$

Single Displacement Reaction

A more reactive element displaces or substitutes a less reactive element from its compound.

A+BC→B+AC

Here, A is more reactive than B and it substitutes B from its compound.

e.g. $Zn + 2HCl \rightarrow H_2 + ZnCl_2$

Double Displacement Reaction

You may have already guessed. This can be imagined as an exchange of partners.

One element from one compound combines with an element from the other compound.

The second element from the first compound combines with the second element from the second compound.

For ionic compounds, the positive ion in the first compound combines with the negative ion in the second compound, and the positive ion in the second compound combines with the negative ion in the first compound.

AB+CD→AD+BC

e.g. $HCl + NaOH \rightarrow NaCl + H_2O$

REDOX Reaction

RedOx = Reduction and Oxidation.

In terms of oxygen or hydrogen transfer

- Oxidation is gain of oxygen or loss of hydrogen

- Reduction is gain of hydrogen or loss of oxygen

E.g. $Fe_2O_3 + 3CO \rightarrow 2Fe + 3CO_2$

'Fe_2O_3' loses its oxygen atom, forming 'Fe' and hence, it is reduced.
On the other hand, 'CO' gains an oxygen atom, forming 'CO_2'. Therefore, it is oxidised.

E.g. $2NH_3 + 3Br_2 \rightarrow N_2 + 6HBr$

'NH_3' loses its hydrogen, forming 'N_2'. Therefore, it is oxidised.
'Br_2' gains hydrogen, forming 'HBr'. Therefore, it is reduced.

In terms of electron transfer

- Oxidation is the loss of electrons

- Reduction is the gain of electrons

The easiest way to remember this is by: **OIL RIG**

OIL:
Oxygen **I**s **L**oss of electrons

RIG:
Reduction **I**s **G**ain of electrons

Example:
$CuO + Mg \rightarrow Cu + MgO$

Reactants:
The oxidation state of Cu: +II
The oxidation state of O: -II
The oxidation state of Mg: 0

Products:
The oxidation state of Cu: 0
The oxidation state of O: -II
The oxidation state of Mg: +II

Writing out the ionic equation of this, we get:
$Cu^{2+} + Mg \rightarrow Cu + Mg^{2+}$

In this reaction, Cu gains electrons because its oxidation number decreases from +II to 0. So, it is reduced, as Reduction is the gain of electrons.

In this reaction, Mg loses electrons because its oxidation number increases from 0 to +II. So, it is oxidised, as oxidation is the loss of electrons.

Since both reduction and oxidation occurs in this reaction, it is a REDOX reaction.

Disproportionation Reactions
In a disproportionation reaction, the same species is both oxidised and reduced.

Example:
$Cl_2 + H_2O \rightarrow HCl + HClO$

Oxidation state of Cl in Cl_2 = 0
Oxidation state of Cl in HCl = -1
Oxidation state of Cl in HClO = +1

Therefore, Cl is both **reduced and oxidised**.

Oxidising and Reducing Agents

- An oxidising agent is a substance, which oxidises something else.

- A reducing agent is a substance, which reduces something else.

Let us take the example that we used above.

$CuO + Mg \rightarrow Cu + MgO$

As we discussed,
Cu is being reduced in this reaction. However, the substance that is reducing it is the Mg. Therefore, Mg is the reducing agent.

Similarly, Mg is being oxidised in the above reaction. The substance that is oxidising is Cu. Therefore, Cu is the oxidising agent.

Conclusion:
An oxidising agent oxidises something else, but it itself is reduced.
A reducing agent reduces something else, but it itself is oxidised.

This may seem confusing but it is crucial that you understand the concept.

Neutralisation Reaction

Neutralisation occurs when an acid reacts with a base. `

You may wonder what the difference is between an alkali and a base. An alkali is basically a base, which is soluble in water. Not all bases are soluble but the ones that are soluble are called alkali.

Acid in solution produces H^+ ions.
Alkali in solution produces OH^- ions.

$H^+ + OH^- \rightarrow H_2O$

A neutral pH substance (pure water) is formed when an alkali (soluble base) reacts with an acid.
A salt is also formed.

Chemistry - Reactivity Series and Displacement Reactions

The reactivity series is a list of elements placed in the order of their reactivity. The most reactive element is placed at the top and the reactivity decreases down the list.

It would be ideal if you remember the following reactivity series. You would not be given any information of reactivity of elements in the exam.

Lithium —————— Most reactive in this reactivity series
Potassium
Sodium
Lithium
Calcium
Magnesium
Aluminium
Zinc
Iron
Copper
Silver
Gold
Platinum —————— Least reactive in this reactivity series

Try making a sentence with the first letter of each element in the above reactivity series. It will help you remember the series.

Chemistry - Equilibria

A reversible reaction is one in which there is both a forward reaction (reactants are made into products) and a reverse reaction (products are broken to form reactants).

The sign '$\rightleftharpoons$' is used to show that the reaction is reversible.

Example:
$N_2 + 3H_2 \rightleftharpoons 2NH_3$

Reversible reactions always result in a mixture of reactants and products being formed.

Reversible reactions in a closed system reach equilibrium when the rates of forward and reverse reactions are constant.

There are three factors that can affect the equilibrium position:

- Temperature

- Pressure

- Concentration

Temperature
You first need to know whether heat is given out or taken in.

Example:
$A + B \rightleftharpoons C + D \qquad \Delta H = -200 \text{ kJ mol}^{-1}$

The negative sign in the '-200' shows that the forward reaction (reactants forming products) is exothermic (heat if given out).
The reverse reaction would be the same except that heat would be taken in i.e. ΔH = '+200'. **If**

temperature is increased
According to According to Le Chatelier's law, the position of equilibrium will move to counteract the change. The position of equilibrium will move so that temperature is reduced.

If temperature is increased, the system would need to absorb more heat. Therefore, heat would need to be taken in. This would favour the endothermic reaction. Therefore, the position of equilibrium would shift to the left.

Therefore, A and B would be produced.

If temperature is decreased
According to According to Le Chatelier's law, the position of equilibrium will move to counteract the change. The position of equilibrium will move so that temperature is increased.

If temperature is decreased, the system would need to give out more heat. Therefore, heat would need to be given out. This would favour the exothermic reaction. Therefore, the position of equilibrium would shift to the right.

Therefore, C and D would be produced.

- Increasing the temperature favours the endothermic reaction since heat would need to be taken in.

- Decreasing the temperature favours the exothermic reaction since heat would need to be given out.

Pressure

This only applies to reactions involving gases.

Example:

A+2B⇌C+D

If pressure is increased

According to According to Le Chatelier's law, the position of equilibrium will move to counteract the change. The position of equilibrium will move so that pressure is reduced.

Number of moles on the left:
No. of moles of A = 1
No. of moles of B = 2
Total no. of moles on the left = 1 + 2 = 3

Number of moles on the right:
No. of moles of C = 1
No. of moles of D = 1
Total no. of moles on the right = 1 + 1 = 2

Increasing the pressure favours the reaction, which produces lesser moles of gases. Since number of moles produced is lesser in the forward reaction, the forward reaction is favoured. So C and D would be produced.

If pressure is decreased

According to According to Le Chatelier's law, the position of equilibrium will move to counteract the change. The position of equilibrium will move so that pressure is increased. This can happen by producing more molecules.

Number of moles on the left:
No. of moles of A = 1
No. of moles of B = 2
Total no. of moles on the left = 1 + 2 = 3

Number of moles on the right:
No. of moles of C = 1
No. of moles of D = 1
Total no. of moles on the right = 1 + 1 = 2

Decreasing the pressure favours the reaction, which produces more moles of gases. Since number of moles produced is more in the reverse reaction, the reverse reaction is favoured. So A and B would be produced.

Concentration

According to Le Chatelier's law, if the concentration of a substance is changed, the equilibrium will shift to minimise the effect of that change.
If we add a chemical that is present on either side of the reaction equation, this will cause a shift in the equilibrium position.

Example:

A+B⇌C+D

Let us increase the concentration of B.
According to the law, the position of equilibrium will shift to counteract this change. It will have to shift in such a way, that the concentration of B decreases again.
It will react with A to turn it into C + D.
The position of equilibrium moves to the **right** (towards the products).

Similarly, if we decrease the concentration of A, the equilibrium will move to the left (towards the reactants) to increase the concentration of A.

Catalysts

Adding a catalyst has **NO EFFECT** on the position of the equilibria.

This is because a catalyst speeds up the forward and the reverse reaction to the same extent.

A catalyst can only speed up reactions.

Chemistry - Oxidation Numbers

Oxidation numbers are given to an element in a compound, such that the sum of oxidation numbers of the compound's constituent elements is equal to the charge on the compound.

Elements	Oxidation Number
Group 1 metals	+I
Group 2 metals	+II
Oxygen	-II, except in peroxides (-I)
Hydrogen	+1
Fluorine	-I
Chlorine	-I

Example:
Let us consider the following compound:

- H_2SO_4

Find the oxidation state (number) of sulphur.

Hydrogen usually has oxidation number (+1)
There are two hydrogen atoms so we have $(+1 \times 2) = +2$

Oxygen usually has oxidation number (-2)
There are four oxygen atoms, so we have $(-2 \times 4) = -8$

The charge on the compound is 0.

So we must satisfy the equation:
Ox no. of H + Ox no. of O + Ox no. of S = 0
$2 + (-8) + $ Ox no. of S = 0
$-6 + $ Ox no. of S = 0
Ox no. of S = +6

Example:
Let us consider the following compound:

- MnO_4^{-1}

Find the oxidation state (number) of manganese in the above compound.

Oxygen usually has oxidation number (-2)
There are four oxygen atoms, so we have $(-2 \times 4) = -8$

The charge on the compound is -1.

So we must satisfy the equation:

Ox no. of O + Ox no. of Mn = -1
(-8) + Ox no. of Mn = -1
-8 + Ox no. of Mn = -1
Ox no. of Mn = +8 – 1
Ox no. of Mn = +7

Oxidation number of an element on its own is always zero (0).

Example:
Oxidation number of 'Na' in Na = 0
Oxidation number of 'O' in O_2 = 0
Oxidation number of 'H' in H_2 = 0

Chemistry - Moles

A mole is the mass of a substance that contains 6.02×10^{23} particles of that substance.
Symbol: **n**
SI unit: **mol**

Example:
1 mol of carbon-12 has a mass of 12 grams and contains 6.02×10^{22} of carbon atoms.

To find the number of moles of a substance, we need to use the following formula:
Number of moles = Mass of substance ÷ Mr of the molecule
n = M ÷ Mr

In the above equation,

- Mass is a straightforward quantity measured in grams (g)

- Mr is the sum of the relative atomic masses (Ar) of each constituent atom present in the molecule. It is measured in arbitrary units or grams per mol (g mol⁻¹). **You will be given the Ar of each of the atoms present in the molecule in the exam.**

Example:
Find the number of moles in 10 grams of H_2O.
(Ar of H = 1, O = 16)

We first need to find Mr of H_2O.
There are two atoms of Hydrogen.
Ar of each atom of H = 1. Ar of two atoms of H = 1 x 2 = 2
There is one atom of Oxygen. Ar of each atom of O = 16.
Mr of H O = 2 + 16 = 18

We are given the mass = 10 g
n = M ÷ Mr
n = 10 ÷ 18
n = 0.5555 ≈ 0.56 mol

You can rearrange the formula to make (M) or (Mr) the subject of the formula.

- $M = n \times Mr$

- $Mr = M \div n$

Questions can also involve calculating moles from concentration and volume. If we are given the concentration and volume of a substance, then we can calculate the mole with the following equation:

Moles = Concentration x Volume
$n = c \times v$

Majority of the times, the volume will be given in **cm³** and the concentration will be given in **mol dm⁻³**. You will have to convert the volume given into **dm³**.

To convert cm³ to dm³, we need to divide the volume by 1000.
100 cm³ = 0.1 dm³
25 cm³ = 0.025 dm³
50 cm³ = 0.05 dm³

Example:
You are given a 25 cm³ sample of HCl of concentration 0.02 mol dm⁻³. Find the moles of HCl present.

We are given the concentration and the volume of HCl.
We first need to convert the 25 cm³ to dm³.
25 cm³ = 0.025 dm³

$n = c \times v$
$n = 0.02 \times 0.025 = 0.0005$ mol

You can rearrange the formula to make concentration or volume the subject of the formula.

- $c = n \div v$

- $v = n \div c$

Chemistry - Molar Ratios

Molar ratio questions are very common in BMAT exams. This involves the use of Moles and Reaction equations.

It is best to use an example to understand molar ratios.

Example 1:

Sodium reacts with water to form sodium hydroxide and water. 4.76 grams of sodium hydroxide was formed. Find the mass of sodium used.

$2Na + 2H_2O \rightarrow 2NaOH + H_2$
(Ar of Na = 23, O = 16, H = 1)

We first need to find the Mr of NaOH.
$(23 \times 1) + (16 \times 1) + (1 \times 1) = 23 + 16 + 1 = 40$

$n = M \div Mr$
$n = 4.76 \div 40 = 0.119$

The reaction equation above shows that 2 moles of Na forms 2 moles of NaOH (highlighted in red colour).

Molar ratio = 2 : 2 = 1 : 1
Therefore, moles of Na used = 0.119

Using the formula $M = n \times Mr$
$M = 0.119 \times 23 = 2.737 \text{ g} \approx 2.74 \text{ g}$

Example 2:

50 cm³ of ammonia of concentration 0.3 mol dm⁻³ reacts with oxygen to form nitrogen gas and water. Calculate the moles of nitrogen gas formed.

$4NH_3 + 3O_2 \rightarrow 2N_2 + 6H_2O$

Convert 50 cm³ to 0.05 dm³
Moles of ammonia used = concentration x volume
$n = c \times v$
$n = 0.05 \times 0.3 = 0.015 \text{ mol}$

Molar ratio of Ammonia : Nitrogen gas = (4 : 2) = (2 : 1)
2 moles of ammonia form 1 mole of nitrogen gas. So moles of nitrogen gas produced would be half of the moles of ammonia produced.

So moles of nitrogen gas produced = ½ x 0.015 = 0.0075 mol

Chemistry - Chemical Bonding, Structure and Properties

Atoms react to form compounds to completely fill their outer shell with electrons. We can say that they need to attain the electronic configuration of noble gases because noble gases (Group 18 elements) have full outer shells.

There are three types of bonding you need to know for the BMAT:
1) Ionic bonding
2) Covalent bonding
3) Metallic bonding

The type of bonding taking place depends on the atoms involved in the reaction.

Ionic Bonding

Ionic bonds form when there is a large, uneven sharing of electrons. This happens due to the large difference in electronegativities of the elements involved in the bonding.
Electronegativity refers to the measure of the tendency of an atom to attract a bonding pair of electrons.

Ionic bonds **usually** form between a metal and a non-metal, although not always with a large difference in electronegativity.
A good example of this is Sodium chloride.

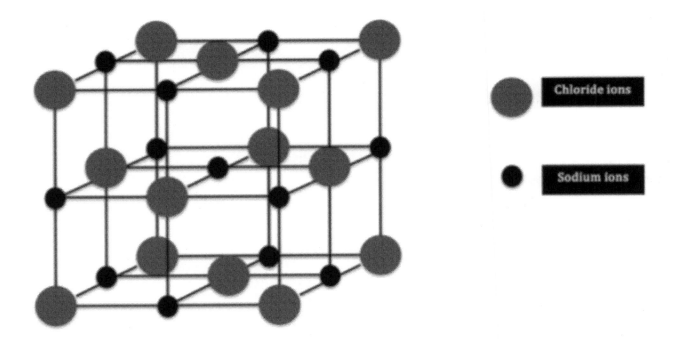

In sodium chloride, chlorine has a much greater electronegativity than sodium. This allows chlorine to pull the bonding electrons towards it completely. It gains an electron and forms the negative chloride ion.

Sodium, hence, loses an electron to form a positive ion.

From the diagram, it can be seen that ions are arranged into a 3D ionic lattice of positive and negative ions.

Covalent Bonds

A covalent bond is formed when two atoms share a pair of electrons. It mostly occurs in non-metal elements.

The shared electrons are in the outer shells of the atoms. Each atom contributes one electron to the shared pair of electrons in a covalent bond.

Dot and cross diagrams can be used to show covalent bonding.
E.g. this is the bonding present in a molecule of methane. Note that only electrons in the outer shell of each atom are shown.

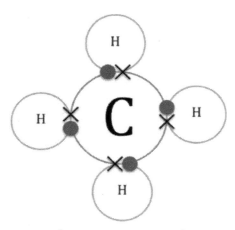

Carbon forms a covalent bond with each Hydrogen atoms. Therefore, in total, carbon forms 4 covalent bonds. This allows carbon to fill its outer shell and each hydrogen atom to fill its outer shell.

Some molecules require double bonds (such as carbon dioxide) or triple bonds (nitrogen molecule).

In the diagram below, you can see that each oxygen atom forms two covalent bonds to fill their outer shell and the carbon atoms four covalent bonds in total to fill its outer shell.

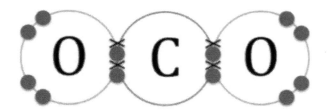

Properties of Simple Covalent Structures

Simple covalent structures only contain a few numbers of atoms. They are very small.

1) Low melting and boiling points T
his is because the **intermolecular** forces between simple molecules are very weak. Therefore, they require little energy to break these forces. Hence, their melting and boiling points are very low. It is important that you understand that intermolecular forces are broken and **NOT** intramolecular forces.

2) Do not conduct electricity
In order to conduct electricity, a substance needs to contain charged particles or have free electrons, which can move from place to place. However, this is not the case with simple molecules. Hence, simple molecules cannot conduct electricity even when liquid or in water.

Properties of Giant Covalent Structures

Giant covalent structures contain a large number of atoms, joined by covalent bonds. In this section, we will discuss the properties of diamond and graphite, as they are the main giant covalent structures you need to know for BMAT.

Diamond

In diamond, each carbon atom is joined to **four other carbon atoms** by strong covalent bonds. The carbon atoms form a tetrahedral network structure.

There are **no free electrons**.

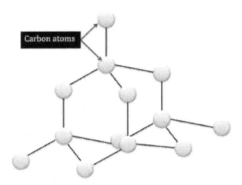

Properties of Diamond

1) The presence of strong covalent bonds makes the diamond very hard.
2) Very high melting point due to the presence of strong covalent bonds.
3) Does not conduct electricity since there are neither charge particles nor free electrons.

Graphite

In graphite, each carbon atom is joined to three other carbon atoms by covalent bonds.
The carbon atoms form layers of hexagonal rings.
There are no covalent bonds between the layers.
One delocalised electron is present from each atom.

Properties of Graphite

1) The presence of weak forces between the hexagonal layers allows graphite the layers to slide over each other. This makes graphite slippery. Hence, it can be used as lubricants.

2) Graphite can conduct electricity due to the presence of delocalised electrons.

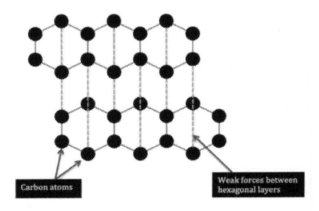

Chemistry - Electrolysis

Electrolysis is a process in which electrical energy breaks down electrolytes, using direct current supply. Electrolytes are ionic compounds, which are either in a **molten state** (heated to become liquids) OR **dissolved in water**.

The free-moving ions in the electrolytes are attracted to the oppositely charged electrodes, which connect to the direct current supply.

An **electrode** is a solid electric conductor that carries current into non-metallic solids, liquids, or gases. **The**

Electrodes

The **cathode** is the negatively charged electrode. This means that positive ions (**cations**) move towards the cathode. The cations receive electrons (**reduction**) to change into atoms or molecules.

The **anode** is the positively charged electrode. This means that negative ions (**anions**) move towards the anode. The anions lose electrons (**oxidation**) to form atoms or molecules.

Why is Direct current used in Electrolysis?

Direct current (DC) is used in electrolysis. Alternating current (AC) is not used. This is because DC provides a one-way flow of electrons, which is appropriate for electrolysis.

If AC were used, energy would be transferred through the back and forth movement of electrons. However, in electrolysis, electron current is required to move in one direction only.

Electrolysis of Brine

Brine is a high-concentration solution of sodium chloride and water. Reaction equations:

Cathode: $2H^+ + 2e^- \rightarrow H_2$

Anode: $2Cl^- \rightarrow Cl_2 + 2e^-$

Overall process: $2NaCl + 2H_2O \rightarrow Cl_2 + H_2 + 2NaOH$

The OH^- ions remain in the solution. The solution becomes alkaline because there are more OH^- ions than H^+ ions

Preferential Discharge of Ions

When more than one type of cation or anion is present in a solution, only one cation or anion are selectively discharged.

In order to predict which ions will be discharged, we need to consider the following three factors:
1) The **position** of metal (producing the cations) in the reactivity series
2) The **concentration** of ions in the electrolyte/solution
3) The **nature** of electrodes

Electroplating using copper (copper sulphate)

Electroplating involves putting a thin layer of metal onto a metal object. This requires the use of electrolysis.

We can use electroplating to purify copper.

The cathode is pure copper.
The anode is impure copper
The electrolyte is copper (II) sulphate solution

When DC is supplied, copper ions from the electrolyte gain electrons to become copper atoms at the **cathode**.
Equation: $Cu^{2+}(aq) + 2e^- \rightarrow Cu(s)$

At the **anode**, copper atoms lose electrons and become copper ions in the electrolyte.
Equation: $Cu(s) \rightarrow Cu^{2+}(aq) + 2e^-$

Chemistry - Empirical Formula

The empirical formula of a compound is the simplest **whole number** ratio of atoms of each element in the compound.

For example,
The empirical formula of C_4H_8 is CH_2.
Similarly, the compound, which has the empirical formula CH_2, could have the molecular formula C_2H_4, C_3H_6, C_4H_8 etc.

Calculating Empirical Formula

You will either be given the **masses** of individual elements or **percentage** of elements present in a compound.

Example:
A compound contains 40% carbon, 6.7% hydrogen and 53.3% oxygen.

i) Find the empirical formula of the compound.
ii) After finding the empirical formula, find the molecular formula of the compound if the Mr of the compound is 180.

(Ar of C = 12, H = 1, O = 16)

Solution:

Firstly, we divide the percentages of elements with their respective Ar.

$40 \div 12 = 3.3$
$6.7 \div 1 = 6.7$
$53.3 \div 16 = 3.3$

We then divide each of the values obtained above by the lowest value obtained. The lowest value obtained above is 3.3

$3.3 \div 3.3 = 1$ (Carbon)
$6.7 \div 3.3 \approx 2$ (Hydrogen)
$3.3 \div 3.3 = 1$ (Oxygen)

The ratio of Carbon : Hydrogen : Oxygen = 1 : 2 : 1

Hence, the empirical formula is CH_2O

ii) Mr of CH_2O = (12) + (1 x 2) + (16) = 30
Mr of compound = 180
Ratio = 180 ÷ 30 = 6

So we need to multiply the ratios of individual elements in CH_2O by 6.
This will give us = $C_6H_{12}O_6$

Chemistry - Percentage Yield

Yield is the amount of product.
Theoretical yield is the amount of product expected to form based on stoichiometric calculations.
Actual yield is the amount of product that is actually formed after carrying out a reaction.

Formula:

Percentage yield = (Actual Yield ÷ Theoretical yield) x 100

Example:

After a reaction, the actual yield of a product = 7.2 grams. The percentage yield is 36%. What is the theoretical yield?

0.36 = 7.2 ÷ Theoretical Yield
Theoretical Yield = 7.2 ÷ 0.36 = 20 grams

Example:

$KClO_3$ decomposes according to the following equation:
$2KClO_3 \rightarrow 2KCl + 3O_2$

10 grams of $KClO_3$ decomposes.

(Ar of K = 39, Cl = 35.5, O = 16)

a) Calculate the theoretical yield of KCl to the nearest whole number
b) Calculate the percentage yield of KCl if actual yield is 4 grams

Solution:

a) Mr of $KClO_3$ = (39) + (35.5) + (16 x 3) = 122.5
Moles = 10 ÷ 122.5 ≈ 0.08
Molar ratio of $KClO_3$: KCl = 2 : 2 = 1 : 1
Moles of KCl = 0.08 mol
Mr of KCl = 39 + 35.5 = 74.5
Mass of KCl = 74.5 x 0.08 = 5.96 grams ≈ 6 grams (this is the theoretical yield)

b) Percentage yield = (4 ÷ 6) x 100 = 66.7%

Chemistry - Energetics

When a reaction occurs, energy is transferred to or from the surroundings. However, energy is conserved in chemical reactions. This means that the total amount of energy in the universe remains the same before and after the reaction.

Endothermic Reactions

Endothermic reactions are those in which energy is taken **in** from the surroundings. This causes the temperature of the surrounding to decrease.
E.g. thermal decomposition reactions
You can identify an endothermic reaction if the ΔH value is positive.
E.g. A + B → C   ΔH = +239
You can also tell that a reaction is endothermic if energy profile of the reaction is like this:

Endothermic Reaction Energy Profile

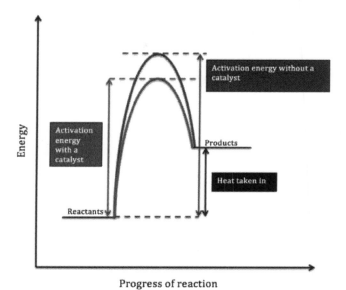

Progress of reaction

Exothermic Reactions

Exothermic reactions are those in which energy is given **out** to the surroundings. This causes the temperature of the surrounding to increase.

E.g. combustion reactions

You can identify an exothermic reaction if the ΔH value is negative.

E.g. $A + B \rightarrow C$ $\qquad$ $\Delta H = -239$

You can also tell that a reaction is exothermic if energy profile of the reaction is like this:

Exothermic Reaction Energy Profile

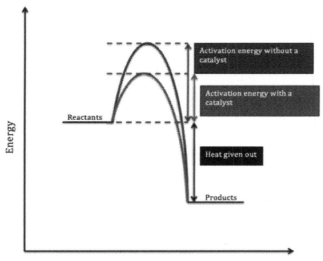

Progress of reaction

Breaking and Making Bonds

There is a transfer of energy when bonds are broken or are formed. We can identify endothermic or exothermic reactions by looking at the energy required to break existing bonds in reactants and energy required to make new bonds in products.

In order to break bonds, energy is taken in from the surroundings.
When new bonds are formed, energy is given out to the surroundings.

A reaction is **exothermic** if more energy is released in making new bonds in products than is taken in when breaking bonds in reactants.

A reaction is **endothermic** if more energy is taken in to break bonds in reactants than is given out when forming new bonds in products.

Chemistry - Group Chemistry

Group 1 (Alkali metals)

Group 1 elements (alkali metals) are highly reactive. These metals donate electrons to form positive ions (cations). They only contain 1 electron in their outermost shell. They lose this outermost electron to gain a charge of +1.

These metals are soft and have **relatively low melting and boiling points**.

Since alkali metals are highly reactive, they must be stored in oil to prevent them from reacting with air.

Trends in group 1:

– Atomic radius increases
– Electronegativity decreases
– Reactivity increases
– Melting point and Boiling point decreases

Reactions

- **With water**
  Group 1 metals react with water to form **metal hydroxides** and **hydrogen gas**. e.g.
  $Na + H_2O \rightarrow NaOH + H_2$

- **With oxygen**
  Group 1 metals react with water to form **metal oxides**.
  e.g. $4Na + O_2 \rightarrow 2Na_2O$

- **With halogen**
  Group 1 metals react with a halogen to form an ionic salt. This reaction gets more vigorous and exothermic as we go down the group.
  e.g. $Na + Cl \rightarrow NaCl$

Group 17 (Halogens)

Halogens are the most reactive non-metals. They accept electrons to form negatively charged ions (anions). They have 7 electrons in their outermost shell. They accept 1 electron to obtain a charge of -1.

Trends in group 17:

– Atomic radius increases
– Electronegativity decreases
– Reactivity decreases
– Melting point and Boiling point increases

Silver Nitrate Test

If we want to identify the halide in an unknown solution, we use the silver nitrate test.

1) The solution is first acidified with dilute nitric acid.
2) Add dilute silver nitrate solution to the sample.

Silver ions react with halide ions to form insoluble precipitates.

If **Chloride** is present, a **White** precipitate is formed.
If **Bromide** is present, a **Cream** precipitate is formed.
If **Iodide** is present, a **Yellow** precipitate is formed.

Group 18 (Noble gases)

Noble gases are the least reactive elements in the Periodic Table. This is because they have the maximum number of electrons in their outer shell. Therefore, they rarely react with other elements since they are already stable.

e.g. Helium's outermost shell can hold only 2 electrons and Helium has 2 electrons in its outermost shell.
Neon can hold 8 electrons in its outermost shell. Its configuration is 2,8. Therefore, its outermost shell is full.

Transition Elements (d-block elements)

The transition elements are the elements between Group 2 and Group 13.

Transition elements can form different stable ions. For example, Iron can have ions Fe^{2+} and Fe^{3+}. Similarly, Copper can form Cu^+ and Cu^{2+}.

They can also form coloured compounds. For example, copper sulphate has a distinct blue colour.

Transition metals also play an important role of catalysts in many reactions. For example, Iron is used as a catalyst in the Haber process.

Chemistry - Polymers

Polymers are long-chain molecules, which can either occur naturally or be made by chemical processes.

Alkenes or other unsaturated molecules with a C=C bond will react with each other to form long-chain saturated molecules called **polymers**.
This is known as **polymerisation**. The individual molecules that react together to form polymers are called **monomers**. Since many molecules join together to form a single product, this is an example of an **addition reaction**.

Many monomers → One polymer

How To Form A Polymer When The Monomers Are Given?

1) Change the double bond in the monomers to single bonds
2) Join the monomers

Polymers are very large molecules compared with other molecules.
A **repeat unit** is the part of a polymer, which can make a complete polymer if many of them were joined from end to end.

Polymerisation

Repeating unit of polyethene

Polyethene

In the diagram above, you can see how 4 ethene molecules underwent polymerisation to form polyethene.
The repeat unit is ethene without a double bond. We can call Polyethene an **addition polymer**.

How To Identify The Monomer In A Given Polymer?

1) Identify all the groups of atoms present in the polymer
2) Identify how often they appear and after how many carbon atoms

Example:
Find the monomer in the following polymer:

$$
\begin{array}{cccccc}
H & H & CH_3 & H & H & H \\
| & | & | & | & | & | \\
-C & -C & -C & -C & -C & -C- \\
| & | & | & | & | & | \\
CH_3 & H & H & H & CH_3 & H
\end{array}
$$

In this, you can see that CH_3 is a special group of atoms present. It appears after every 2 carbon atoms. So the answer would be:

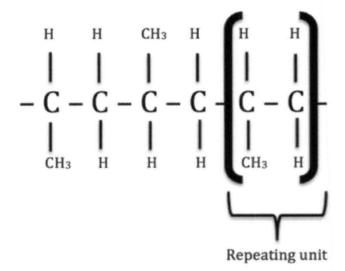

Repeating unit

However, this is not the monomer. The monomer would be propene with formula:
$CH_3 - CH = CH_2$

Chemistry - Separation Techniques

Chemical procedures can be used to separate compounds and mixtures.

We can separate compounds using chemical reactions either displacement reactions or electrolysis.

-Displacement reactions have been covered in another topic in this course 'Reactivity Series and Displacement Reactions.'

-Electrolysis is covered in the topic 'Electrolysis.'

Mixtures
Chemical procedures are also capable of separating mixtures. A **mixture** contains substances, which may be mixed together but cannot be chemically joined.

Miscible Liquids
Miscible liquids are those, which can be mixed easily with or without stirring.
Such liquids need to be separated using fractional distillation.
In fractional distillation, miscible liquids can be separated since they have different boiling points.

Paper chromatography
Paper chromatography can be used to separate non-volatile liquids.

It relies on two different 'phases':

1) **The stationary phase**: paper chromatography is uniform, absorbent paper.
2) **The mobile phase**: solvent moves through the paper, carrying different substances with it.

You also need to know the use of Rf values.

Rf Values Rf values can be used to identify unknown chemicals if they can be compared to a range of reference substances.

Rf is calculated using the following equation:
Rf = (distance travelled by substance) ÷ (distance travelled by solvent)

Example:

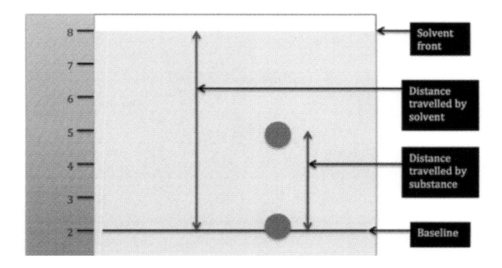

In the paper chromatography above, distance travelled by solvent = 8 – 2 = 6 cm
Distance travelled by substance = 5 – 2 = 3 cm Rf = 3 ÷ 6 = 0.5

Rf values vary from 0 to 1. They cannot be below 0 or above 1.

Immiscible Liquids

Immiscible liquids are those, which will not mix at all even with stirring. An example of an immiscible liquid mixture is oil and water. They do not mix.

Such liquids are separated using a separating funnel. Each layer of liquid needs to be removed one at a time.

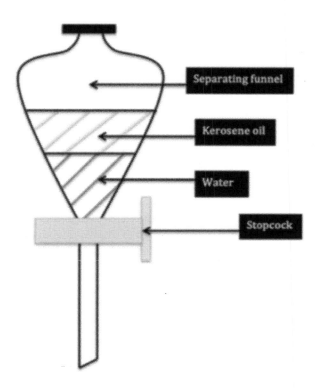

Soluble Solids Mixed with Insoluble Solids

Let us say we need to separate a mixture of two solids (one soluble and one insoluble).

The mixture is first added to water. The soluble solid will **dissolve** whilst the insoluble solid will not. We can then **filter** the insoluble solid.

The soluble solid can then be obtained by **evaporating** the water.
We can also use **distillation** to separate the soluble solid from the water.

Physics - Electricity

Questions from electricity are common in the BMAT exams. They have appeared numerous times and I am sure that you may have come across some if you have done some past papers.

Even though you may have studied electricity before, it is important to start from the basics just to jog your memory.

Quantity	Symbol	SI Unit
Current	I	Amperes (A)
Voltage	V	Volts (V)
Power	P	Watts (W)
Charge	Q	Coulombs (C)
Resistance	R	Ohms (Ω)
Time	t	Seconds (s)

Here are some common electricity equations:

Current = Charge ÷ Time (**I = Q ÷ t**)
Voltage = Current x Resistance (**V = I x R**)
Power = Voltage x Current (**P = I x R**)

Example: Charge = 200 C Time = 10 s Resistance = 20 Ω

1. Find the current

2. Find the voltage

3. Find the power

The only way to find the current from the information given is to use the equation (I = Q ÷ t).
I=200÷10I=20A

To find the voltage, we use the formula V = I x R
V = 20 x 20 V = 400 V

To find the power, we use the formula P = I x V
P = 20 x 400 P = 8000 W

You may be asked to determine whether a certain quantity can be equal to a certain equation.

Example
Prove that P = I²R

Firstly, we know that P = IV
We also know that V = IR
If we substitute (V = IR) into the equation (P = IV), we get the following:
P = I x (IR)
P = I x I x R
P=I²R

Physics - Circuits

A circuit is a closed loop in which electrons can travel in.

Components of a circuit:

Cell or a Battery (many cells):
This provides a voltage to get the current flowing in a circuit.

Voltmeter:
It is an instrument used for measuring the potential difference between two points in an electric circuit.

Ammeter:
It is an instrument used for measuring current in an electric circuit.

Resistor:
Resistors are used to reduce current flow.

Lamp:
A lamp is used to determine whether or not electricity is flowing.

Switch:
A switch is used to turn the flow of electricity on or off.
In an open switch, the wire is not connected. Therefore, no electricity flows if the switch is open.
In a closed switch, the wire is connected. Therefore, electricity flows if the switch is closed.

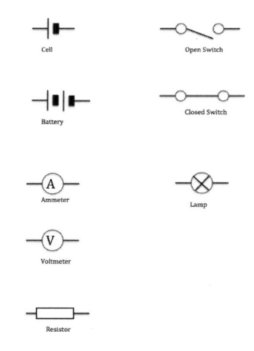

Components of circuit

Series Connections
If components are connected one after the other in the same loop, then the circuit is in series.

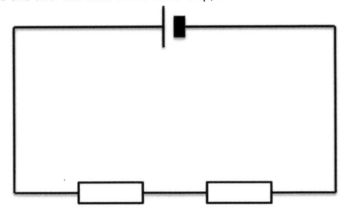

Resistors are in series

In the above circuit, the resistors are placed one after the other. Therefore, they are said to be in series.

Voltage in Series Circuits
The potential difference (voltage) across both resistors must add up to give the potential difference of the battery.

Let us say voltage across the first resistor (R_1) = A
Let us say voltage across the second resistor (R_2) = B
Therefore, voltage across battery = A + B

Let us say voltage across first resistor (R_1) = 4 V
Let us say voltage across second resistor (R_2) = 8 V
Therefore, voltage across battery = 4 + 8 = 12 V

Current in Series Circuits
The current across both resistors will be the same.
Current R_1 = Current R = Current across battery

Let us say current across first resistor (R_1) = 4 A
Then, current across second resistor (R_2) = 4 A
Therefore, resistance of circuit = 4 A

Resistance in Series Circuits
To calculate the total resistance of the circuit, we add the resistance of each of the resistors.

Let us say resistance of first resistor (R_1) = A
Let us say resistance of second resistor (R_2) = B
Therefore, resistance of circuit = A + B

Let us say resistance of first resistor (R_1) = 4 Ω
Let us say resistance of second resistor (R_2) = 8 Ω
Therefore, resistance of circuit = 4 + 8 = 12 Ω

Parallel Connections
In a parallel circuit, the current divides into two or more paths before recombining to complete a circuit.

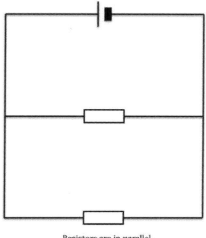

Resistors are in parallel

In the above circuit, there are two branches, each with one resistor.

Voltage in Parallel Circuits
The potential difference (voltage) across both resistors is equal. The potential difference across the battery is equal to the potential differences across each of the resistors.

Let us say voltage across first resistor (R_1) = A
Then, voltage across second resistor (R_2) = A
Therefore, voltage across battery = A
Voltage across R_1 = Voltage across R_2 = Voltage across battery

Let us say voltage across first resistor (R_1) = 4 V
Then, voltage across second resistor (R_2) = 4 V
Therefore, voltage across battery = 4 V

Current in Parallel Circuits
However, the sum of the currents across R_1 and R_2 is equal to the current across the battery.

Let us say current across first resistor (R_1) = A
Let us say current across second resistor (R_2) = B
Therefore, current across battery = A + B
Current across R_1 + Current across R_2 = Current across battery

Let us say current across first resistor (R_1) = 4 A
Let us say current across second resistor (R_2) = 8 A
Therefore, current across battery = 8 + 4 = 12 A

Resistance in Parallel Circuits
Let total resistance = R_x
To calculate the resistance of the circuit, we use a formula:
$$\frac{1}{R_x} = \frac{1}{R_1} + \frac{1}{R_2}$$
Let resistance of R_1 = 4 Ω
Let resistance of R_2 = 8 Ω
$\frac{1}{R_x} = \frac{1}{4} + \frac{1}{8} = \frac{3}{8}$
$R_x = \frac{3}{8}$
$R_x = 2.666 \approx 2.67$ Ω

Physics - Transformers

A **transformer** is a device that can change the potential difference of an alternating current.
There are two types of transformers:
- Step-up transformers: increase the voltage
- Step-down transformers: decrease the voltage

Step-Up Transformer
A step-up transformer has fewer turns on its primary coil and more turns on its secondary coil.
This allows it to increase the voltage of the alternating current.

Step-Down Transformer
A step-down transformer has more turns on its primary coil and fewer turns on its secondary coil.
This allows it to decrease the voltage of the alternating current.

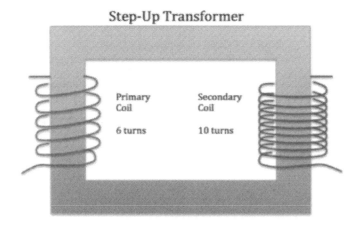

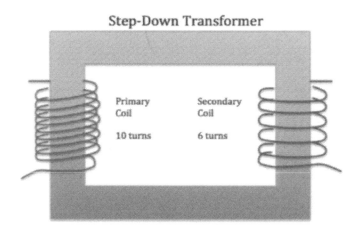

Transformers formula:
The ratio of potential differences must match the ratio of the number of turns on its primary and secondary coils.

$$\frac{V \text{ (primary coil)}}{V \text{ (secondary coil)}} = \frac{\text{number of turns on the primary coil}}{\text{number of turns on the secondary coil}}$$

$$\frac{V(p)}{V(s)} = \frac{N(p)}{N(s)}$$

Example:
A transformer has 24 turns on its primary coil. Its primary voltage is 12 V and its secondary voltage is 400 V.
Find the number of turns on its secondary coil.

$$\frac{V(p)}{V(s)} = \frac{N(p)}{N(s)}$$

$(12 \div 400) = (24 \div$ number of turns on secondary coil)
Number of turns on secondary coil $= (24 \times 400) \div 12$
Number of turns on secondary coil $= 800$

Efficiency of a transformer:
If a transformer is 100% efficient, it means that there is a total transfer of electrical power.
This gives rise to the formula:
Current (primary) x Voltage (primary) = Current (secondary) x Voltage (secondary)
$$I(p) \times V(p) = I(s) \times V(s)$$

Example:
A 100% efficient transformer has 1000 turns in its primary coil and 250 turns in its secondary coil. The current in the secondary coil is 40 A. What is the current in its primary coil?

Solution:
We need to use both of the following formulae to solve this:
$$I(p) \times V(p) = I(s) \times V(s)$$

$$\frac{V(p)}{V(s)} = \frac{I(s)}{I(p)}$$

Using the ratio of turns formula:
$$\frac{V(p)}{V(s)} = \frac{N(p)}{N(s)}$$

$$\frac{I(s)}{I(p)} = \frac{N(p)}{N(s)}$$

$$\frac{40}{I(p)} = \frac{1000}{250}$$

$$I(p) = 10 \text{ A}$$

Physics – Newton's 3 Laws of Motion

First Law

An object will remain at rest or in uniform **motion** in a straight line unless acted upon by an external force.

e.g. if a car is at rest, then it will remain at rest until a force is exerted on it by either the engine or a person trying to push it.
If a car is moving at a constant velocity, then it will continue to do so until the engine applies more or less force on it, causing it to either accelerate or decelerate.

Second Law

The rate of change of momentum is directly proportional to the force applied, and this change in momentum takes place in the direction of the applied force.

$\Delta p \propto F$

e.g. If you use the same amount of force to move a bicycle and a car, the bicycle would have more acceleration because it has a smaller mass compared to a car.

Third Law

If a body A exerts a force on body B, then body B will exert an equal and opposite force on body A.

e.g. A standing person of mass 70 kg exerts a force of 700 N on the ground (their weight). The ground will then exert an equal and opposite force on the person (-700 N).

Physics - Force and Free Fall

A force is a push, pull or a twist.

- Formula: Force = mass x acceleration (F = m x a)

- The unit of force is Newton (N).
  1 Newton is defined as the force that would give a mass of 1 kg an acceleration of 1 m/s².
  $1 N = 1 kg\ m/s^2$

- Force is a **vector** quantity. This means that it has magnitude and direction. Since it has direction, it can either be positive and negative.

Example:
A car, weighing 500 kg, has a constant acceleration of 2 m/s². What is the force produced by its engine? Using the formula F = ma,
F = 500 x 2
F = 1000 kg m/s² = 1000 N

Resultant Force ($\sum F$)
Resultant force is the sum of forces acting on a body.
Let us say two people were pushing a box from opposite directions. One person applies a force of 20 N and the other person applies a force of 10 N.

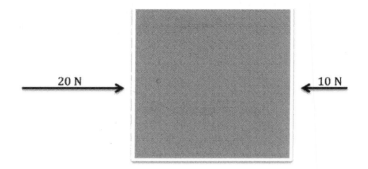

The person applying a force of 10 N is doing it in the opposite direction of the other person. Since force is a vector quantity, the person applying the force of 10 N would have a negative value (i.e. -10 N).

$\sum F = [20 + (-10)] = (20 - 10) = 10$ N to the right

Weight
The weight of a body or an object is also a force. The weight is measured in Newtons.
In order to measure your weight, you must take your mass in kilograms and multiply it by 10. This is because the acceleration of gravity on Earth is 10 m/s².

Let us say a person's mass is 60 kg.
Weight (Force) = Mass x Gravitational acceleration
Weight = 60 x 10
Weight = 600 N

Every object and person on Earth has mass and hence a weight.

Remember:
Acceleration due to gravity on different planets and other Celestial objects have a different value. Moon's acceleration due to gravity is 6 times less than Earth's.
Therefore, a person weighing 600 N on Earth weighs 100N on Moon.
However, a person's mass remains the same. A person who has a mass of 60 kg on Earth will have a mass of 60 kg on Moon.

Free Fall
Free fall is when a person or an object moves downward under the force of gravity only.

The best and most popular example of free fall is a skydiver.

As soon a skydiver jumps out of the plane, the only force acting on him/her is gravity. The person falls with an acceleration of 10 m/s². There is a constant gain of velocity.

If a person weighs 90 kg, their downward force would be their weight, i.e. 900 N.

The increase in velocity is accompanied by an increase in air resistance. Air resistance acts against the force of gravity. Using Newton's third law of motion, air resistance has an equal but opposite force on the person. Air resistance = -900 N

Resultant Force ($\sum F$) = 900 + (-900) = 900 - 900 = 0

Once the magnitude of air resistance becomes equal to the magnitude of the force of gravity, i.e. $\sum F = 0$, the person's acceleration becomes zero and they move downward with constant velocity. This is known as **terminal velocity**.

When the skydiver opens their parachute, the force of air resistance greatly increases as it acts on a much larger surface area (a parachute is very big). This air resistance overwhelms the force of gravity. This causes the skydiver to slow down.

As the skydiver begins to slow down, the air resistance also decreases until the skydiver reaches a terminal velocity again.

A graph of a free fall looks like this:

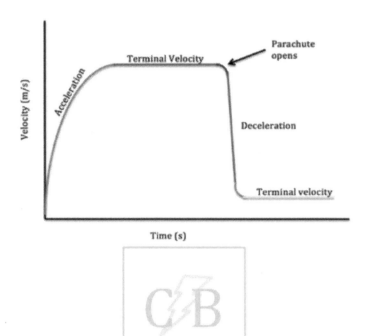

Example:
A skydiver of mass 50 kg opens his parachute and the magnitude of air resistance becomes 800 N. What is the size of acceleration? What is the direction of acceleration?

Solution: Skydiver's weight = 50 x 10 = 500 N
Force downwards = 500 N
Force upwards = 800 N

Net force = 800 + (-500) = 800 – 500 = 300 N

Upward force > Downward force.
Therefore the **direction of acceleration would also be upwards**.

We know F = ma
a = F ÷ m

Net force = 300 N
m = 50 kg
a = 300 ÷ 50 = 6 m/s²

Size of acceleration = 6 m/s²
Direction of acceleration = Upwards

Physics - SUVAT Equations

SUVAT Equations are equations of motion. They are really helpful to solve problems relating to displacement, time, velocity etc.

SUVAT stands for:

- s = Displacement or Distance (m)

- u = Initial velocity (m/s)

- v = Final Velocity (m/s)

- a = Acceleration (m/s²)

- t = Time (s)

Here are the equations:

- $v = u + at$

- $v^2 = u^2 + 2as$

- $s = ut + \frac{1}{2}at^2$

- $s = \frac{1}{2}(u + v)t$

- $s = vt - \frac{1}{2}at$

You must remember these equations, as you will not be given these in the exam. Also, you need to ensure you use the appropriate equation for the problem.

Example:

A car travels at 10 m/s and then accelerates to a constant velocity of 20 m/s. How much time will it take to travel 100m?

You are given:
u = 10
v = 20
s = 100

We are not given acceleration. Therefore, the only appropriate equation to use is 's = ½ (u + v) t)'.
We must rearrange this equation to give 't'.

$s = \frac{1}{2}(u + v)t$
$[2s \div (u + v)] = t$
$t = [2(100) \div (20 + 10)]$
$t = [200 \div 30]$
$t = 6.666 \approx 6.7$ seconds

You can easily rearrange the formulas accordingly to solve the questions.

Physics - Energy

Work Done

When a force, **F**, causes an object to move, work is done on the object by the force. If the object moves by a certain distance, **d**, then the work is calculated as:

W = F x d, in which:
The unit of W is Joules (J)
The unit of F is Newtons (N)
The unit of d is metres (m)

When work is done, energy is transferred from one body to another. So we can say:

Energy transferred = work done

Example:
A man applies a force of 12 N on a cupboard to move it by a horizontal distance of 7.5 m. Calculate the work done.

W = F x d
W = 12 x 7.5
W=90J

Energy and Power

When work is done, a transfer of energy occurs.
Power is the **rate** at which this energy is transferred.

Power = Work done ÷ time
P = W ÷ t, in which:
The unit of P is Watts (W)
The unit of W is Joules (J)
The unit of t is seconds (s)

Example:
A box weighs 4 N. An electric motor is used to lift this box through a vertical height of 24 m. If the box does this in 12 seconds, i) Calculate the work done ii) Calculate the power of the motor.

i) W = F x d
W = 4 x 24
W=96J

ii) P = W ÷ t
P=96÷12
P=8W

Kinetic Energy

Bodies, which are in motion, have kinetic energy.
Formula for Kinetic Energy:
Kinetic Energy = ½ (mass of body) x (velocity)^2
KE = ½mv^2

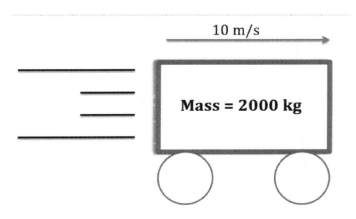

Consider the above vehicle. It has a mass of 2000 kg and it is moving at a velocity of 10 m/s. Its

KE = ½ (2000) (10)²
KE = ½ (2000) (100)
KE = 1000 (100)
KE = 100000 Joules or 100 KJ

Potential Energy

As an object is moved above the ground, it gains gravitational potential energy.
The amount of energy it gains depends on:
- The object's mass (m) in kilograms (kg)
- The height (h) above the ground in metres (m)
- The acceleration due to gravity (g)

The formula for gravitational potential energy:

GPE = mass x height x acceleration due to gravity
GPE = mgh

The acceleration due to gravity on Earth is **10 m/s²**. Other celestial objects such as the Moon or other planets have a different value for the acceleration due to gravity.

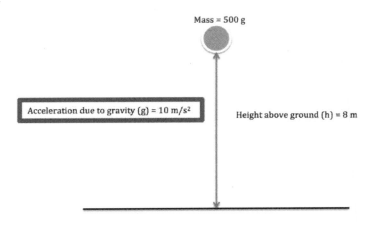

In the above diagram, the ball moves 8 m above the ground. It has a mass of 500 g (0.5 kg). The value of g is 10.

GPE of ball = 0.5 x 8 x 10
GPE = 4 x 10
GPE=40J

KE to GPE and GPE to KE

Let us say a ball is hanging in the air. It will have the maximum GPE possible for the height.

If the ball is cut loose, it will fall downwards due to gravity. Since it will start moving downwards, it will start to gain some **kinetic energy**.
Therefore, some of the GPE will be transferred to KE.

Similarly, if an object is thrown upwards, it will have some KE. When it reaches its highest possible point, all of its KE will be transferred to GPE.

For a split second, it will have no KE and maximum GPE. As soon as it starts falling, it will start to lose GPE and gain KE.

Question relating to KE and GPE are usually asked in conjunction with SUVAT Equations.

Example:
A person throws a ball upwards with a velocity of 12 m/s.
I) Calculate the height that it will reach after 2 seconds.
II) Calculate its GPE at that height if its mass is 400 g.

Solution:
The best way to start answering a question like this is to write down the information given to you and the information that you already know.

We are given:
Initial velocity (u) = 12
Time (t) = 2

We know:
Acceleration (due to gravity) = -10
The acceleration is negative because the ball is moving upwards and the action of gravity is actually downwards.

I) We can use the equation: $s = ut + \frac{1}{2}at^2$ s
$= 12 (2) + \frac{1}{2} [-10 (2)^2]$
$s = 24 + \frac{1}{2} [-40]$
$s = 24 + (-20)$ s
$= 4$ metres

II) We know:
Mass = 400 g = 0.4 kg
Height = 4 metres
Value of g = 10
GPE = 0.4 x 4 x 10 = 1.6 x 10 = 16 Joules

Physics - Energy Conversion

There are many types of energy such as electrical energy, nuclear energy, heat energy, light energy etc. Energy can be converted from one form to another.

Law of Conservation of Energy

"The law of conservation of energy states that energy can neither be created nor destroyed. It can only be **transferred** from one form to another."

Energy Efficiency

No device, which changes energy from one form to another, is perfect.
Take the example of a light bulb. It is supplied with electrical energy so it can transfer this electrical energy to light energy.
However, not all electrical energy it receives is converted to light energy. Some of this electrical energy is converted to unwanted heat energy too. Therefore, some energy is wasted as heat energy.

A very efficient device will waste little energy whilst an inefficient device will do the opposite.

We can calculate the percentage efficiency of a device.
Percentage Efficiency = (Useful energy ÷ Total energy supplied) x 100

Example:
A bulb is supplied with 90 J of energy. Out of this, only 45 J is usefully transferred. Calculate the bulb's efficiency.

Percentage efficiency = (45 ÷ 90) x 100 = 50%

Physics - Momentum

Momentum is defined as the quantity of motion that a body has.
It is measured as the product of its mass and its velocity.

Momentum = Mass x Velocity
p = m x v
Mass – kg
Velocity – m/s
Momentum – kg m/s

Since velocity is a vector quantity (it could have a negative value), momentum is also a vector quantity, meaning that it can also be negative.

Example:

A truck of mass 2 tonnes is moving at a velocity of 45 km/h. Find its momentum.
Solution: Mass = 2 tonne = 2 x 1000 kg = 2000 kg
Velocity = 45 km/h = (45 x 5) ÷ 18 = 12.5 m/s
p = m x v
p = 2000 x 12.5
p = 25,000 kg m/s

Conservation of Momentum

"For two bodies, A and B, colliding in an isolated system, the total momentum before and after the collision is conserved."

A popular example of this is a car crash.
Imagine two cars travelling in opposite directions towards each other. Each car would have its own momentum.
When they crash with each other, the sum of their momentums before the collision would be equal to the sum of their momentums after the collision.
It would be simpler if we use an example.

Collide and Lock
Objects that were moving separately before the collisions stick, and move off together after the collision.

Example:
Two cars, A and B are travelling towards each other.
A has a mass of 200 kg and a velocity of 10 m/s.
B has a mass of 400 kg and a velocity of 8 m/s.
I) Calculate their individual momentums
II) Calculate their momentums after the collision

After the collision, the cars stick together and move as one.
III) Calculate the velocity of both cars after the collision.

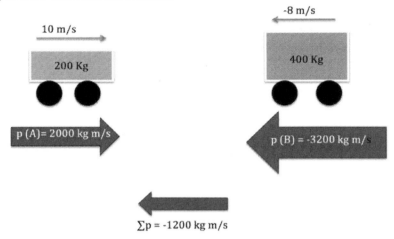

Solution (I):
Momentum of A = 200 x 10 = 2000 kg m/s
Since B is travelling in the opposite direction, its velocity would be negative.
Momentum of B = 400 x (-8) = -3200 kg m/s

Solution (II):
Sum of momentum before collision = p(A) + p(B)
∑p = p(A) + p(B) = 2000 + (-3200) = -1200 kg m/s
According to the law of conservation of momentum,
Total momentum before collision = total momentum after collision So
total momentum after collision = -1200 kg m/s

Solution (III):
Momentum is conserved.
Since the cars stick together, their velocity would be v (AB).
Mass (AB) = 200 + 400 = 600 kg
∑p = m (AB) x v (AB)
-1200 = 600 x v (AB)
v (AB) = -1200 ÷ 600
v (AB) = -2 m/s
The negative sign indicates that both cars are moving from right to left.

Collide and Split

Objects, which were moving separately before the collisions, move off separately after the collision.

Example:

A ball (X) of mass 200 g collides with a stationary ball (Y) of mass 150g with a velocity of 2.5 m/s. X moves with a velocity of 1 m/s after the collision. Find the velocity of Y after the collision.

Conservation of momentum

$m_1v_1 + m_2v_2 = m_1v_1 + m_2v_2$
$(0.2 \times 2.5) + (0.15 \times 0) = (0.2 \times 1) + (0.15 \times v_2)$
$0.5 = 0.2 + (0.15 \times v_2)$
$0.3 = (0.15 \times v_2)$
$v_2 = 2$ m/s

Explosions

In an explosion, there is no initial momentum as nothing is moving. After the collision, objects move off in separate directions.

Example:

A cannon of mass 2000 kg fires a cannonball of mass 20 kg. The initial velocity of the cannonball is 50 m/s. Calculate the recoil velocity of the cannon.

Conservation of momentum

$m_1v_1 + m_2v_2 = m_1v_1 + m_2v_2$

Since momentum before collision = 0, 0
$= m_1v_1 + m_2v_2$
$0 = (2000 \times v_1) + (20 \times 50)$
$0 = (2000 \times v_1) + 1000$
$-1000 = (2000 \times v_1) v_1$
$= -0.5$ m/s

(Note: The negative sign on the velocity indicates that the cannon moves in the opposite direction to the cannonball)

Physics - Stopping Distances

Stopping distances refer to the shortest distance within which a driver must bring their vehicle to a stop in an emergency.

Stopping distance = thinking distance + braking distance

The **thinking distance** refers to the distance a vehicle travels in the time it takes for the driver to apply their brakes after realising they need to stop. This depends upon the driver's **reaction time**.

The **braking distance** refers to the distance vehicle travels after the brakes have been applied.

Example:

A truck, of mass 1000 kg, has a velocity of 12 m/s. The driver's reaction time is 0.4 s. The braking force is 4000 N. What is the stopping distance?

Solution:
Thinking distance = 12 x 0.4 = 4.8 m

$KE = \frac{1}{2}mv^2 = 0.5 \times 1000 \times (12)^2 = 72,000$ J
$W = \frac{1}{2}mv^2 = 72,000$ J
$F \times d = 72,000$
d (braking distance) = 72,000 ÷ 4,000 = 18 m

Stopping distance = 18 + 4.8 = 22.8 m

Physics - Motion Graphs

You may be asked to identify certain aspects of a motion graph.
The graph can be either one of these:
- Velocity – Time Graph
- Displacement – Time Graph
- Acceleration – Time Graph

Velocity – Time Graph

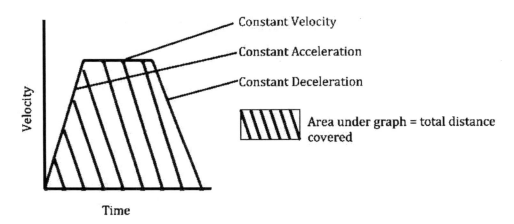

Velocity-time graphs have the following components:
- Constant Velocity, shown by the flat line on the graph
- Constant Acceleration, shown by the upward line on the graph
- Constant Deceleration, shown by the downward line on the graph
- Area under graph = total distance covered

The first three points are straightforward.
The fourth point may be slightly tricky. You may be asked to calculate the total distance covered by a vehicle. The graph shown above is shaped like a trapezium. You will be given the values on the graph. You can then use the area of trapezium formula to find the area under the graph. This will give you the total distance travelled by the vehicle.

The graphs can be of different shapes too, not just trapezium-shaped.

Displacement – Time Graph

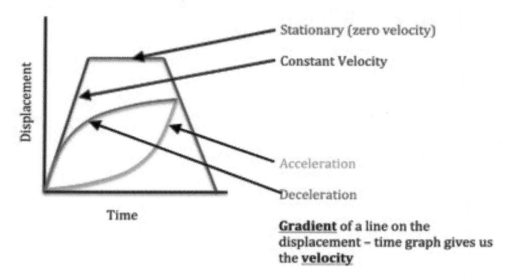

The displacement – time graphs could have the following components:
- **Stationary phase**. Since, displacement is constant, the body is not in motion. Therefore, it is at rest.

- **Constant positive velocity**. The displacement is increasing proportionally. Therefore, the velocity is increasing at a constant rate.

- **Constant negative velocity**. The displacement is decreasing proportionally. Therefore, the velocity is decreasing at a constant rate.

- Also, it is important to note that when displacement becomes zero, Since displacement is a vector quantity, this shows that the body returns to its original starting position.

- **Acceleration**. The displacement is increasing at an increasing rate. Therefore it must be accelerating.

- **Deceleration**. The displacement is decreasing at an decreasing rate. Therefore it must be decelerating.

- The gradient of any line on the graph give us the value of the **velocity**.

Acceleration – Time Graph

There is not much they can ask you about acceleration-time graphs.

The flat line shows constant acceleration. This means that the body is accelerating at a constant rate.

The dashed line shows that the body begins to move at a constant velocity. Since the velocity becomes constant, i.e. velocity remains same, acceleration suddenly drops to zero.

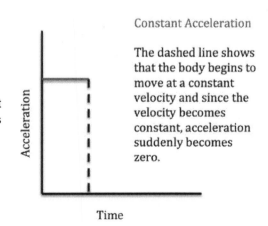

Constant Acceleration

The dashed line shows that the body begins to move at a constant velocity and since the velocity becomes constant, acceleration suddenly becomes zero.

Physics - Waves

Waves are vibrations that transfer energy without any matter (solid, liquid or gas) being transferred.
E.g. light and sound travel as waves.

Waves have the following components:
- Amplitude
- Wavelength
- Time period
- Frequency

Amplitude (A) is the maximum displacement moved by a point on a wave from its equilibrium position. It is measured in **metres (m)**.

Wavelength (λ) is the distance between two successive crests or troughs of a wave. It is measured in **metres (m)**.

Time period (T) is the time taken for one complete cycle of vibration to pass in a given point. It is measured in **seconds (s)**.

Frequency (f) is the number of waves that pass a fixed point in a given amount of time. It is measured in **Hertz (Hz)**.

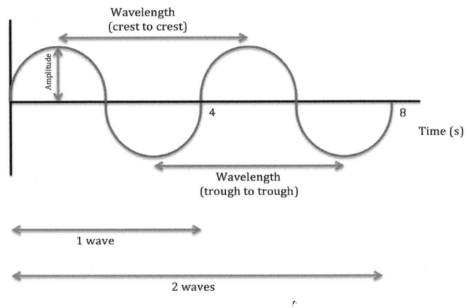

Relationship between **Frequency (f)** and **Time period (T)**:
- **T=$^1\!/f$**
- **f=$^1\!/$T**

In the above wave diagram,
T = 4 seconds
f = ¼ = 0.25 Hz

Types of Waves
There are two types of waves.

Transverse Waves
In transverse waves, the vibrations are at **right angles** to the direction of travel of wave.
E.g. Light and other electromagnetic radiation

Longitudinal Waves
In longitudinal waves, the vibrations are **parallel** to the direction of travel of wave.
E.g. Sound waves

Wave Speed
The speed of a wave is related to its frequency and wavelength. It is measured in **(m/s)**.

Wave speed = Frequency x Wavelength
$v = f \times \lambda$

E.g. A wave of frequency 2000 Hz has a wavelength of 2 m. Calculate its speed.
v = 2000 x 2 = 4000 m/s

Physics - Sound Waves

Sound waves are produced when an object or substance vibrates. Sound waves can travel through solids, liquids and gases **only**, meaning that they cannot travel through a vacuum.

Properties of Sound Waves
Sound waves are **longitudinal** meaning that the vibrations are in the same direction as the direction of travel.

When sound waves reflect off surfaces, we hear these reflections as **echoes**.
Hard and smooth surfaces are good at producing echoes.
Soft and rough surfaces are good at absorbing sound, which is why they do not produce lots of echoes. **Speed of sound in air = 343 m/s**

Ultrasound
Human beings can hear sound of frequency as low as 20 Hz and as high as 20,000 Hz.

Sound, which has a frequency higher than 20,000 Hz, is called ultrasound. This is too high pitched for humans to hear but other animals can bear this sound.

Some Uses of Ultrasound
1) Health check of unborn babies
2) SONAR
3) Clean jewellery
4) Physiotherapy

Physics - Reflection, Refraction & Total Internal Reflection

Reflection
Waves can be reflected at a surface.

Law of Reflection:
Angle of incidence = Angle of Reflection

In reflection, there are two rays: the incident ray and the reflected ray.
Normal is an imaginary line, which is perpendicular to the surface.

The angle of incidence is measured between the incident ray and the normal.
The angle of reflection is measured between the reflected ray and the normal.

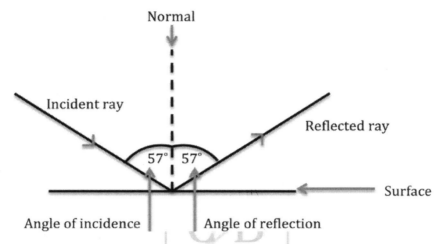

In the image, you can see that the angle of incidence (angle between the incident ray and the normal) is 57°.
Therefore, the angle of reflection (angle between the reflected ray and the normal) is also 57°.
The normal is the dashed line 90° to the surface.

Refraction
When light travels from one medium (e.g. air) to another medium (e.g. glass), its **speed** changes. This causes its **direction** in the second medium to change as well.
Look at the diagram below:

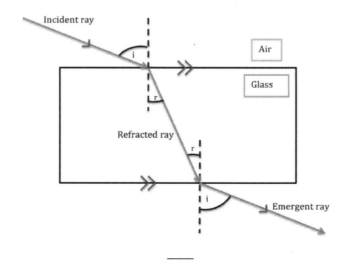

The incident ray's direction changes when it travels from air to glass.

When light travels from a less dense medium such as air to a denser medium such as glass, its **speed decreases**. This causes the light to bend towards the normal (as seen in the diagram). Therefore,

Angle of incidence (i) > Angle of refraction (r)

When light travels from a denser medium such as glass to a more less medium such as air, its **speed increases**. This causes the light to bend away from the normal (as seen in the diagram).

The emergent ray bends away from the normal when the light travels from the glass back into the air.

Total Internal Reflection
At a certain angle of incidence, the refracted ray of light travels along the boundary of the two media.

This angle of incidence is called the **critical angle**. The critical angle is different for every medium.

For glass, the critical angle is 42°.

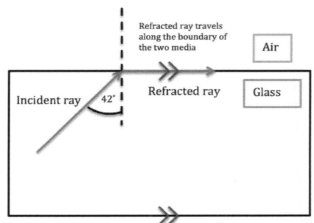

If the angle is increased further than the critical angle, then the light will be totally internally reflected.

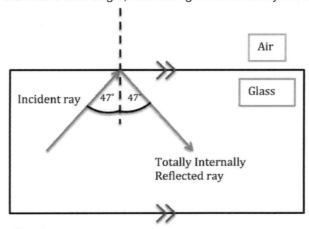

Conditions for Total Internal Reflection:

1) Light must be travelling from a denser medium to a less dense medium

2) The angle of incidence must be greater than the critical angle.

Physics - Electromagnetic Spectrum

The electromagnetic spectrum is a continuous range of wavelengths. Different parts of the spectrum have different uses and dangers. These uses and dangers are dependent on their wavelength and frequency.

Nature and Properties of Electromagnetic Waves

All electromagnetic waves:
1) can transfer energy as radiation
2) can travel through a vacuum
3) can travel at speed of light in a vacuum (300,000,000 m/s)
4) are **transverse waves** which means their vibrations are at right angles to the direction of wave travel

Parts of EM Spectrum

1) Radio waves
2) Microwaves
3) Infrared
4) Visible light
5) Ultraviolet
6) X-rays
7) Gamma rays

These can be distinguished by different wavelengths and frequencies.

Radio waves have the **longest wavelengths** and **lowest frequencies**.
Gamma rays have the **shortest wavelengths** and **highest frequencies**.

Wavelength decreases as we move from radio waves to gamma rays.
Frequency increases as we move from radio waves to gamma rays.

Uses

- **Radio waves**: broadcasting and communications

- **Microwaves**: cooking food

- **Infrared**: night vision equipment

- **Visible light**: human sight, photography (only part of the spectrum which we can see)

- **Ultraviolet**: fluorescent lamps

- **X-rays**: medical use (in X-rays)

- **Gamma rays**: sterilising food and medical equipment

<u>**Dangers**</u>

- **Radio waves**: no damage if absorbed by the human body

- **Microwaves**: internal heating of body cells

- **Infrared**: can cause burns to the skin

- **Visible light**: no damage if absorbed by the human body

- **Ultraviolet**: cause burns on the skin and even cancer

- **X-rays**: lead to mutation in human cells causing cancer

- **Gamma rays**: lead to mutation in human cells causing cancer

---

Physics - Conduction, Convection & Radiation

Energy can be transferred by 3 methods: Conduction, Convection, and Radiation.

<u>Thermal Conduction</u>

Thermal energy can be transferred from one place to another place by conduction. It is transferred by microscopic collisions of particles and movement of electrons within a material. Heat is transferred from the hot end of the object to the cold end.

A thermal conductor is a material, which can allow thermal energy to be transmitted through it easily. E.g. metals

A thermal insulator is a material, which reduces the heat transfer between objects.
E.g. gases and non-metals.

<u>Electrical Conduction</u>

Movement of electrically charged particles through a medium.

An electrical conductor is a material, which can allow electrical energy to be transmitted through it easily. E.g. silver, aluminium, copper

An electrical insulator is a material, which reduces the electrical energy transfer between objects. E.g.
glass, air, plastic

<u>Factors Affecting The Rate of Conduction</u>

1. Type of material

2. Thickness of material

3. Area of Material

Convection

When a fluid (gas or liquid) is heated, it travels away from the source and carries thermal energy with it. Heat energy is transferred from hot places to cooler places.

Liquids and gases expand when they become hot. Hence, they take up more volume.

The formula: Density = Mass/Volume suggests that Density is inversely proportional to Volume. Since volume increases, density decreases.

Therefore, temperature causes the liquid or gas in hot areas to become **less dense.**

Convection Currents

The hot liquid or gas rises into cold areas since it is less dense than cold gas or liquid. The dense, cold liquid or gas then falls into warm areas.

When the hot gas or liquid cools, it sinks again. The cold gas or liquid at the bottom becomes heated by a source and rises to take the place of the cold gas or liquid.

Factors Affecting the Rate of Convection

1. The rate of air movement

2. Body surface area

Radiation

Heat transfer by radiation takes place in the form of electromagnetic waves, mainly in the infrared region.

No particles are involved in heat transfer by radiation, which is why radiation can work even in a vacuum.

Infrared Radiation

Infrared radiation is a type of electromagnetic radiation. All bodies emit and absorb infrared radiation.

It is important for you to know which type of surfaces are good emitter and absorbers of infrared radiation.

Dull or rough surfaces are **good absorbers and emitters** of infrared radiation.

Shiny surfaces are **poor absorbers and emitters** of infrared radiation.

The hotter the body, the more infrared radiation it radiates in a given time.

Factors affecting the rate at which objects transfer energy by heating:

1) Surface area

2) Volume

3) Material of object

4) Nature of surface

Physics - Types of Radiation

There are three types of radiation:

Types of Radiation	What Is It?	What Can Stop It?	Atomic number	Mass number
Alpha (α)	A Helium nucleus (2 neutrons, 2 protons)	A thin piece of paper	2	4
Beta (ß)	A fast moving electron (-1e)	A few millimetres of aluminium	-1	0
Gamma (γ)	Electromagnetic radiation	Few centimetres of lead	0	0

In the exam, you may be asked to identify the correct properties of each type of radiation.

Questions can also be based on certain nuclear reactions.

Example: Alpha decay
Consider the following reaction:

$^{240}Pu \rightarrow {}^{x}U + {}^{4}He$
(atomic number of Pu = 94, U = y, He = 2)
Find the value of 'x' and 'y'.

Solution:
We know 'Pu' decays by alpha decay since a He nucleus is emitted.

The mass numbers must be equal on the LHS and RHS.
Mass number on LHS = 240
Mass number on RHS = x + 4
Mass number on LHS = Mass numbers on RHS
240 = x + 4
x = 240 – 4
x = 236

The atomic numbers must be equal on the LHS and RHS.
Atomic number on LHS = 94
Atomic numbers on RHS = y + 2
Atomic number on LHS = Atomic numbers on RHS
94 = y + 2
y = 94 – 2
y = 92

Example: Beta decay
Consider the following reaction:

$^{234}Th \rightarrow {}^{x}Pa + {}_{-1}ß$

[atomic number of (Th = 90), (Pa = y), (ß = 0)]
Find the value of 'x' and 'y'.

Solution:

We know 'Th' decays by beta decay since a beta particle (electron) is emitted.

The mass numbers must be equal on the LHS and RHS.
Mass number on LHS = 234
Mass number on RHS = x + 0
Mass number on LHS = Mass numbers on RHS
234 = x + 0
x = 234 – 0
x = 234

The atomic numbers must be equal on the LHS and RHS.
Atomic number on LHS = 90
Atomic numbers on RHS = y + (-1) = (y – 1)
Atomic number on LHS = Atomic numbers on RHS
90 = y – 1
y = 90 + 1
y = 91

It is very unlikely that you will be given a reaction with gamma decay as a gamma particle has 0 atomic number and 0 mass number.

You may also be asked to identify the type of decay that occurs in a reaction.

- If the mass number decreases by 4 and the atomic number decreases by 2, the decay is Alpha (α)

- If the mass number remains the same on the LHS and RHS but the atomic number increases by 1, the decay is Beta (ß)

- If there is no change in the mass number and the atomic number, the decay is likely to be Gamma (γ)

Physics - Half-Life

Half-Life is the time taken for the radioactivity of an isotope to be halved.

Example:
The half-life of a substance X is 25 years.
If we take a 10 grams sample of X, then after 25 years, only 5 grams would remain.

Let us say you are given the half-life of a substance and you are asked to find out the remaining amount after a certain amount of time. We use the following formula:

Remaining mass of sample = Original mass of sample ÷ 2^n

Where 'n' is the number of half-lives.

Example:
You have been given a 10 grams sample of isotope X. Its half-life is 4 minutes.
How many grams of the isotope will remain after 20 minutes?

Solution:
Half life = 4 minutes
Time given = 20 minutes
Number of half lives = 20 ÷ 4 = 5 half lives

Using the formula given,
Remaining mass = Original mass ÷ 2^n (n is number of half lives)
Remaining mass = $10 ÷ 2^5$
Remaining mass = 10 ÷ 32
Remaining mass = 0.3125 grams

In the case where we have to find out the number of half-lives when we are given original mass, remaining mass and the time.

Example:
400 g of a sample drops to 50 g after 300 days.
What is the half-life of the sample?

Solution:
Initial mass = 400 g
Mass of sample after 1st half life = 200 g
Mass of sample after 2nd half life = 100 g
Mass of sample after 3rd half life = 50 g

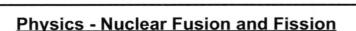

The sample reached a mass of 50 g after 3 half lives.
3 half lives occurred in 300 days.
Time of one half life = 300 ÷ 3 = **100 days**

Physics - Nuclear Fusion and Fission

Nuclear Fusion
In nuclear fusion, two small, light nuclei join together to form one, heavy nucleus.

For the BMAT, you need to know the fusion of hydrogen nuclei to form a helium nucleus.

In stars, two hydrogen nuclei fuse together to form a nucleus of a helium isotope. This occurs under **high temperatures and pressure**.

If deuterium joins with tritium, a helium nucleus and a neutron are emitted.

$$^2H + {}^3H \rightarrow {}^4He + n$$

A high temperature is required to give the hydrogen atoms enough energy to overcome electrical repulsion between the protons.
Nuclear fusion is a very significant process and is a good source of energy.

Nuclear Fission
In nuclear fission, a large atomic nucleus splits into smaller nuclei. It occurs due to the absorption of neutrons.

Fission of U-235 and Chain Reaction

A neutron is absorbed into a uranium-235 nucleus. This causes the nucleus to become uranium-236, which is very unstable.

The U-236 splits into two smaller, daughter nuclei. In addition to these daughter nuclei, two or three neutrons are also emitted. These then collide with other U-235 nuclei to cause further fission reactions.

This is known as a **chain reaction**.

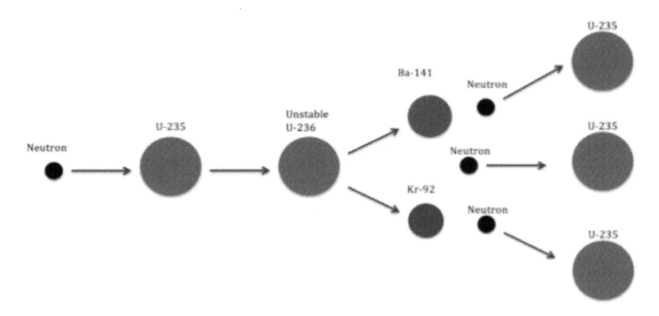

The equation for the above fission reaction would be:

$_1n + _{235}U \longrightarrow _{236}U \longrightarrow _{141}Ba + _{92}Kr$

Physics - Density

The density of an object means how tightly the matter of the object is packed together.
It can also be defined as mass per unit volume.

Density = Mass ÷ Volume
Density = m ÷ V

The unit of density is **kg/m³** or **g/cm³**

Example:
A rock weighing 0.6 kg has a volume of 15 cm³. What is its density?

Solution:
Since the mass is given in kilograms, we need to convert it into grams.
Mass = 0.6 kg = 600 g
Volume = 15 cm³
$\rho = 600 \div 15 = 40$ g/cm³

Example:
A cuboidal block of glass has dimensions 1 m x 60 cm x 2 m. It weighs exactly 2 kg. What is its density?

Solution:
Dimensions of the block = 1 m x 0.6 m x 2 (convert 60 cm to 0.6 m)
Since the block is cuboidal, we can use the formula: (l x b x h) to find the volume.

Volume = (1 x 0.6 x 2)= (2 x 0.6) = 1.2 m³
Mass = 2 kg
ρ = (2 ÷ 1.2) = 1.66666... = 1.67 kg/m³

Physics - Moments

Moment of a force is a measure of its tendency to cause a body to turn about a specific amount.
Moments = Force x Perpendicular distance
M = F x ∟ d
Moments is measured in Newton metre (Nm)

Example:
A force of 20 N acts at a perpendicular distance of 2 m from a pivot. Find the moments.

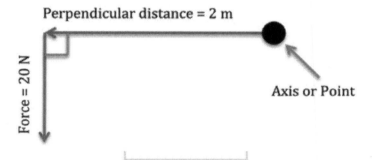

M = F x ∟ d
M = 20 x 2 = 40 Nm

Well as you have already guessed, the questions are not going to be so simple.

Moments question usually involve a beam being balanced on an axis or a point. The beam must be in equilibrium, i.e. totally balanced and not tilting to one side.

In order for the beam to remain completely balanced, one condition is needed to be satisfied:

Clockwise moments = Anti-clockwise moments

Let us understand this with an example.

Example:
A beam is to remain in equilibrium. Here is the diagram:
Find the mass of the beam.

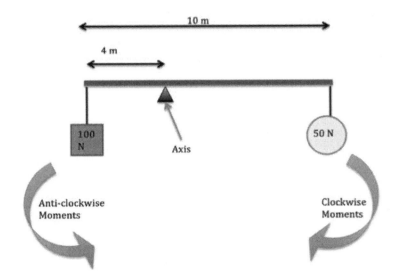

Solution:
Yes! This is a ridiculous question. But don't worry!

Let the mass of beam = K

Anticlockwise moments are the moments of forces trying to move the beam in the anticlockwise direction.
The square is trying to move the beam in an anticlockwise direction.
The square is applying a force of 100 N at a perpendicular distance of 4 m from the axis.

Anticlockwise moments = F x ⌐d
M (Anti-C) = 100 x 4 = 400 Nm

Clockwise moments are the moments of forces trying to move the beam in the clockwise direction. In this case, it is the circle.

However, there is one more force acting in the clockwise direction and you may have guessed it. It is the weight of the beam.
Weight of the beam = mass x g = 10K N (g = 10)

Remember! The weight of a body always acts on its centre (centre of gravity).

Length of beam = 10 m
Centre of beam = 10 ÷ 2 = 5 m
Distance of centre from the axis = 5 – 4 = 1 m
Moment created by weight of beam = 10K x 1 = 10K Nm

Distance of yellow circle from axis = 10 – 4 = 6 m
Moment created by yellow circle = 50 x 6 = 300 Nm
Total M (Clockwise) = 10K + 300

We must satisfy the condition:
Clockwise moments = Anti-clockwise moments
400 Nm = 10K + 300 Nm
100 Nm = 10K
K = 100 ÷ 10 = 10 kg

Physics - Electrostatics

It is important to know that all matter has some charge. It is another matter that atoms have no **overall** charge.

All atoms have electrons and protons. If they have an equal number of protons and electrons, then they become **neutral**.

In this topic, we are going to study how **electrons** can be made to move from one object to another. Note that protons cannot move since they are in the nucleus of each atom.

Examples:
1) Rubbing a plastic rod with a duster
2) Rubbing a rubber balloon on a wool sweater
3) Packing popcorn sticking to your hands

Let us use the first example. When the plastic rod is rubbed, electrons are transferred from the plastic rod to the duster. In the end, the rod has an overall positive charge and the duster has a negative charge.

Static charge occurs when electrons build up on objects.
It can only build up on **insulators** (plastic) and not on conductors (metals).

When a static charge on an object is discharged, electric current flows through the air, causing **sparks**.
Lightning is the result of a large amount of static charge being discharged.

Attraction and Repulsion
You must be familiar with the idea of attraction and repulsion.

Unlike charges attract whilst **like charges repel**.

Protons attract electrons whilst protons repel other protons.
Electrons attract protons whilst electrons repel other electrons.

Uses of Electrostatics

1) Spray painting
2) Photocopiers

Dangers of Electrostatics

1) Touching something with a lot of electric charge can result in an electric shock.
2) Presence of flammable gases, which could be ignited by a spark, causing an explosion.

Maths - Rearranging

Rearranging is a very important topic. You will definitely need it for a lot of questions in Maths, Physics and Chemistry. Maybe even in Biology!

Rearranging basically means making a certain quantity the subject of the formula.

LHS means the left hand side of the equation.
RHS means the right hand side of the equation.

In the equation: $y = mx + c$,
'y' is the LHS (left side of the equal sign)
'mx + c' is the RHS (right side of the equal sign)

Rules:

Make 'a' the subject of the formula in the following equations.

1) $c = b - a$
$c - b = -a$ -a
$= c - b$
(Reverse signs on both sides) a
$= -c + b$
$a = b + c$

2) $c = b + a$
$c - b = a$
$a = c - b$

3) $c = b \div a$
$a = b \div c$

4) $c = b \times a$
$a = c \div b$

5) $c = a \div b$
$a = b \times c$

6) $c = a \times b$
$a = c \div b$

7) c = (-a) x b

-a = c ÷ b

(Reverse signs on both sides) a

= -(c ÷ b)

---

8) 3) c = b ÷ (-a)

-a = b ÷ c

(Reverse signs on both sides)

a = -(b ÷ c)

You may also be asked to rearrange a quantity, which is being square rooted.

c = b + $\sqrt{a}$ $\sqrt{a}$ = c − b

(Square both sides)

$(\sqrt{a})^2 = (c − b)^2$

a = $(c − b)^2 = c^2 - 2bc + b^2$

Complicated Questions

You probably came across some really tough rearranging questions whilst doing past papers. They make look intimidating at first but it is important to do everything step by step.

Do what you can at first and then build up.

Example:

Rearrange the following formula to make 't' the subject of the formula:

a = $\dfrac{\sqrt{(b + t)}}{cd}$

Step 1: Rearrange the denominator 'cd' from RHS to LHS

You get:

acd = $\sqrt{(b + t)}$

Step 2: Square both RHS to LHS

You get:

$(acd)^2 = \{\sqrt{(b + t)}\}^2$

$a^2c^2d^2 = (b + t)$

Step 3: Rearrange 'b' from RHS to LHS

You get:

$a^2c^2d^2 − b = t$

$t = a^2c^2d^2 − b$

Maths - Factorisation and Splitting The Middle Term

Factorisation basically means to take out the common factors in a given equation.

Example:
Factorise the following equation
$x^2 + 2x + x^3$

The common factor in the above equation is 'x'. So we get:
$x (x + 2 + x^2)$

If we open the brackets, we get the original equation.
$x (x + 2 + x^2) = x^2 + 2x + x^3$

Example:
Factorise the following equation
$x^3 + x^2y + 2x^2$

Here, the common factor is x^2. So we get:
$x^2 (x + y + 2)$

Example:
Factorise the following equation
$2x^4 + 4x^2y + 12x^3z$

Here, the common factor is $2x^2$. We get:`
$2x^2 (x^2 + 2y + 6xz)$

Splitting the Middle Term
It is useful to know how to factorise quadratic equations by splitting the middle term. Here is how we do it:

You are given the quadratic equation:
$2x^2 + 11x + 12$

Step 1:
You multiply the third term (+12) with the first term ($2x^2$). We get: $2x^2 \times 12 = 24x^2$

Step 2:
We must split the middle term (11x) into two parts in such a way that the product of the two parts would be $24x^2$ and their sum would be 11x.
The two parts would be: 8x and 3x.
Product of two parts = 8x * 3x = $24x^2$
Sum of two parts = 8x + 3x = 11x

Step 3:
We get the following equation: $2x^2 + 8x + 3x + 12$

Step 4:
We factorise the first two terms and the last two terms. We get: $2x (x + 4) + 3 (x + 4)$

Step 5:
We get a common expression (x + 4) in the equation and the other expression is (2x + 3)

Step 6:
We have factorised the equation! (2x + 3) (x + 4)

Try multiplying the brackets and you will see that: $(2x + 3) (x + 4) = 2x^2 + 11x + 12$

Maths - Power Rules

Rules	Examples
$A^0=1$	$5^0=1$
$A^1=A$	$5^1=5$
$A^2 = (A \times A)$	$5^2 = (5 \times 5) = 25$
$A^3 = (A \times A \times A)$	$5^3 = (5 \times 5 \times 5) = 125$
$A^n = (A \times A \times A \times A \times A...\text{'n'}$ number of times)	$5^n = (5 \times 5 \times 5 \times 5 \times 5...\text{'n'}$ number of times)
$1^n=1$	$1^4=1$
$A^n \times A^a = A^{n+a}$	$5^2 \times 5^3 = (5^{2+3}) = 5^5$
$A^n \div A^a = A^{n-a}$	$5^3 \div 5^2 = (5^{3-2}) = 5^1$
$A^n \div B^n = (A \div B)^n$	$6^3 \div 2^3 = (6 \div 2)^3 = (3)^3 = 9$
$(A^n)^a = A^{n \times a}$	$(5^3)^2 = 5^{3 \times 2} = 5^6 = 15,625$
$A^{n/a} = \sqrt[a]{A^n}$	$5^{3/4} = \sqrt[4]{5^3} = \sqrt[4]{125}$
$A^{-n} = 1/A^n$	$8^{-2} = 1/8^2 = 1/64$
$A^n \times B^n = (A \times B)^n$	$5^3 \times 6^3 = (5 \times 6)^3 = (30)^3$

Maths - Surds

A surd is an expression, which either includes a square root, cube root or any other root symbol. Surds are used to write irrational numbers perfectly, since the decimals of irrational numbers do not terminate or recur.

For example: $\sqrt{2}$ is a surd because its decimal (1.413213…) neither terminates nor recurs.

For the BMAT, you mainly need to learn about surds with square root and cube root.

Rules of Surds

Rule	Example
$\sqrt{a} \times \sqrt{b} = \sqrt{ab}$	$\sqrt{2} \times \sqrt{5} = \sqrt{(2 \times 5)} = \sqrt{10}$
$\sqrt{a} \times \sqrt{a} = a$	$\sqrt{2} \times \sqrt{2} = 2$
$\sqrt{a} \div \sqrt{b} = \sqrt{(a \div b)}$	$\sqrt{6} \div \sqrt{3} = \sqrt{(6 \div 3)} = \sqrt{2}$
$\sqrt{a} + \sqrt{a} = 2\sqrt{a}$	$\sqrt{3} + \sqrt{3} = 2\sqrt{3}$
$\sqrt{a} - \sqrt{a} = 0$	$\sqrt{3} - \sqrt{3} = 0$

Example: Simplify √24

Step 1: First, factorise 24 completely. 24 = 2 x 2 x 2 x 3

Step 2: So √24 = √(2 x 2 x 2 x 3) = √(2^2 x 2 x 3) = √(2^2 x 6)

Step 3: If you have an expression, which is squared (in this case we have 2^2), you can remove it from the square root by removing the square.
√(2^2 x 6) = 2√6

So the answer is 2√6

Example: Simplify $^{10√12}/_{2√28}$

Step 1: Factorise the terms inside the square roots.
√12 = √(2 x 2 x 3) = √(2^2 x 3) = 2√3
√28 = √(2 x 2 x 7) = √(2^2 x 7) = 2√7

Step 2: Multiply the terms outside the square root with their new surds.
10 x 2√3 = 20√3
2 x 2√7 = 4√7

Step 3: Divide the terms outside the square roots
20÷4=5

So the answer is: $^{5√3}/_{√7}$

Example: 2√48 + 29√3 − √108

√48 = √ (2 x 2 x 2 x 2 x 3) = √(2^2 x 2^2 x 3) = 2 x 2√3 = 4√3 2 x 4√3 = 8√3

√108 = √(2 x 2 x 3 x 3 x 3) = √(2^2 x 3^2 x 3) = 2 x 3√3 = 6√3

8√3 + 29√3 − 6√3 = (8 + 29 − 6)√3 = 31√3

The answer is 31√3

Try solving this on your own and then check the solution:

$$\frac{(2\sqrt{3} + \sqrt{3})\ (4\sqrt{3} + 3)}{2\sqrt{3} \times 4\sqrt{3}}$$

Solution:
Solve each term individually.
$(2\sqrt{3} + \sqrt{3})$ = 3√3
$(4\sqrt{3} + 3)$ will remain as it is
$2\sqrt{3} \times 4\sqrt{3}$ = 8 x 3 = 24

So we have:

$$\frac{3\sqrt{3}\ (4\sqrt{3}+3)}{24}$$

$$\frac{3\sqrt{3}\ (4\sqrt{3})+3\sqrt{3}\ (3)}{24}$$

$$\frac{(12\times3)+9\sqrt{3}}{24}$$

$$\frac{36+9\sqrt{3}}{24}$$

Each of these terms is divisible by 3. To simplify further we need divide each term by 3.

36÷3=12
9√3÷3=3√3
24÷3=8

So the final answer is:

$$\frac{12+3\sqrt{3}}{8}$$

Rationalising the denominator

We are given the fraction:

$$\frac{\sqrt{3}}{\sqrt{7}}$$

In order to rationalise the denominator, we need to multiply the numerator and the denominator by the denominator.

Solution:

$$\frac{\sqrt{3}}{\sqrt{7}}\times\frac{\sqrt{7}}{\sqrt{7}}$$

$$\frac{\sqrt{21}}{7}$$

Example: Rationalise the denominator of

$$\frac{5}{3\sqrt{3}}$$

<u>Solution:</u>

$$\frac{5}{3\sqrt{3}} \times \frac{3\sqrt{3}}{3\sqrt{3}}$$

$$\frac{15\sqrt{3}}{27}$$

Exception (Important!)

If the denominator contains a '+' or '-' sign, you need to multiply the numerator and denominator with an expression with a swapped sign.
If the denominator is 3 - √3, you need to multiply the numerator and denominator by 3+√3

Example: Rationalise the denominator of

$$\frac{5}{3 + \sqrt{3}}$$

<u>Solution:</u>

$$\frac{5}{3 + \sqrt{3}} \times \frac{3 - \sqrt{3}}{3 - \sqrt{3}}$$

$$\frac{5\,(3 - \sqrt{3})}{(3 + \sqrt{3})\,(3 - \sqrt{3})}$$

$$\frac{15 - 5\sqrt{3}}{9 - 3}$$

$$\frac{15 - 5\sqrt{3}}{6}$$

Maths - Simultaneous Equations

Simultaneous equations are really straightforward.

You are given two equations:
2x + y = 14
5x + 2y = 30
Find out the values of both 'x' and 'y'.

Step 1:
Choose a variable (either x or y) and make their coefficients in both equations equal. Let us use 'y' for this problem.
In the first equation, coefficient of y = 1
In the second equation, coefficient of y = 2
We must make the coefficient of 'y' in equation one = 2
So we multiply the whole equation one by 2.
We get the following equation:
2 [2x + y = 14]

4x + 2y = 28
Hence, we made the coefficient of y = 2

Step 2:
Rearrange both equations to make '2y' the subject of the formula.
Equation 1: 2y = 28 – 4x
Equation 2: 2y = 30 – 5x

Step 3:
We get:
2y = 28 – 4x = 30 – 5x
28 – 4x = 30 – 5x
-4x + 5x = 30 – 28
x = 2

Step 4:
Substitute the value of (x = 6) in any equation.
2x + y = 14
2(2) + y = 14
4 + y = 14
y = 10

Step 5:
Ensure that you have arrived at the correct answers by substituting the values of 'x' and 'y' in the other equation.
5x + 2y = 30
5(2) + 2(10) = 30
10+20=30

Hence, we have arrived at the correct answer.

Maths - Mean (Average)

You have come across mean throughout your academics. It is a simple concept of finding the average of a set of data.

In the BMAT exam, however, the question is twisted around to confuse the candidates.

Therefore, it is important to brush up on the basics. I created a sample complicated question to give you an idea of how the question can be twisted around.

My advice is to use the information to calculate anything that you can. Then go from there.

Example:
There are three students in Further Maths in Year 12. Their scores in a test are 45, 49 and 52. What is the mean score?

Solution:
We add the scores together first. We get:
45+49+52=146

Then, we divide it by the number of students, i.e. 3
146 ÷ 3 = 48.666 ≈ 48.7

Complicated Question
There is 'P' number of people in a group. They have a mean weight of 50 kg.

The number of people in the group increases by 20 and the mean weight decreases by 2 kg.
Create a formula for mean weight of the second group.

Solution:

First Step
Find the mean weight of the second group.
We are told that the mean weight decreases by 2 kg.
So mean weight = 50 – 2 = 48 kg.

Second Step
Find the number of people in the second group.
We are told that the number of people increases by 20.
So number of people in second group = P + 20

Third Step
Find the sum of the weights of people in the second group.
We can simply do this by multiplying the mean weight (48) with the number of people (P + 20). Total weight of people in second group = 48 (P + 20) = (48P + 960) kg

Fourth Step
Create a formula for the mean weight (48 kg).
Mean weight = total weight ÷ total number of people
48 = (48P + 960) ÷ (P + 20)

Maths - nth Term and Linear Sequences

You are given the following sequence:
3, 6, 9, 12….

In the above sequence, the 1st term is 3, 2nd term is 6 and so on.

However, the question is how do you find the 32nd term of the sequence? (Just an example)

For this, you first need to find the nth term of this sequence.

You probably already realised that the value increases by 3 after every term. So the nth term would be the difference between each term (3 in this case) multiplied by n.

nth term = 3n

To find 32nd term, n must be equal to n.
n = 32
32nd term = 3 x 32 = 96

Similarly, if you are asked to find the 61st term, 61st term = 3 x 61 = 183

Similarly, you are given the following sequence:
4, 9, 14…

In this sequence, the difference between each term is 5. However, in this case, nth term cannot be 5n.

For example, the 4th term in the above sequence should be 19. However, if use 5n, we get 5 x 4 = 20. So this is incorrect.

To find the nth term, we can use the first term as an example.

1st term is 4

Difference between each term = 5
n^{th} term should be = 5n – 1

2nd term = 9
Using 5n – 1, we get = 5 (2) – 1 = 9

Similarly, 6th term would be = 5 (6) – 1 = 29 and so on.

Tricky Sequences

Consider the sequence: 7, 8, 11, 16, 23…

In this sequence, the difference between consecutive terms increases each time.

Difference between 8 and 7 = 1
Difference between 11 and 8 = 3
Difference between 16 and 11 = 5
Difference between 23 and 16 = 7

However, the differences of the differences are constant.
3–1=2
5–3=2
7–5=2

REMEMBER: When the differences keep changing but the differences of the differences remain constant, you use the following formula to find the formula of the nth term

$$ a + (n-1)d + \left[\left(\frac{1}{2}\right)(n-1)(n-2)(c) \right] $$

a = first term
d = difference between first two numbers
n = term number
c = difference of the differences

In this case,
a = 7
d = 1
n = term number
c = 2

So,
n^{th} term = 7 + 1(n – 1) + $\frac{1}{2}$ x 2 (n – 1) (n – 2)
n^{th} term = 7 + n – 1 + n^2 – 3n + 2
n^{th} term = n^2 – 2n + 8

By looking at the sequence you can see that the 6th term should be 23 + 9 = 32

Let try finding the 6th term with the formula.
n = 6
n^2 – 2n + 8
6^2–2(6)+8
36–12+8=32
There you go!

Please, remember this formula for the exam. It looks complicated, but it is not impossible. Keep trying and you will remember it by heart!

Trickiest Example (Past Paper Question)
Try solving this past paper question on your own. Then check the solution given below.

Question:
The sequence is 1, 3, 6, 10….
The difference between the nth and $(n + 3)^{th}$ term is 126. Find the value of n.

Solution:
Sequence = 1, 3, 6, 10
Differences = 2, 3, 4
Differences of the differences = 1, 1

a = 1
d = 2
c = 1

Using the formula given above, Formula for the nth term = 0.5! + ᵗ ‾‾‾‾

Now, we need to find the formula for the $(n + 3)^{th}$ term.
To do this, all you need to do is replace every 'n' in the formula with (n + 3) ‾

We know difference between these two terms is 126

$$\left({}_{6+3.5!+} \underline{\quad} \right) \left(-0.5! + \underline{\quad} \right) = 126$$

6 + 3n − 126
3n = 126 − 6
3n = 120
n = 40

In our past paper worked solutions, there is another method mentioned with which you can solve this question. However, this is the proper way to solve it.

Maths - Surface Areas and Volumes

Question relating to surface areas and volumes are common in BMAT exams.
It is important to know surface areas and volumes of some common shapes.
2-D shapes do not have three dimensions. Therefore, they cannot have a volume.

2D Shapes Formulae:

Shape	Perimeter	Area
Square	4a	a^2
Rectangle	2 (l + b)	l x b
Circle	2πr	$πr^2$
Triangle	Sum of 3 sides	½ (b x h)
Trapezium	Sum of 4 sides	½ (a + b) h

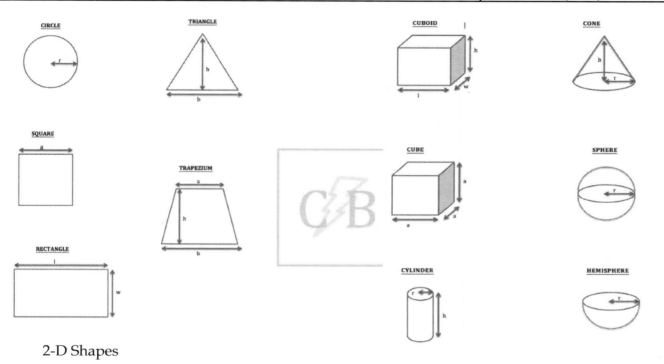

2-D Shapes

3-D Shapes

3-D Shapes Formulae:

Shape	Surface Areas	Volume
Cube	$6a^2$	a^3
Cuboid	2lh + 2wh + 2lw	(l x b x h)
Cylinder	$2πrh + 2πr^2$	$πr^2h$
Cone	$πr [r + \sqrt{(h^2+r^2)}]$	$πr^2(h ÷ 3)$
Sphere	$4πr^2$	$\frac{4}{3}πr^3$
Hemi-sphere	$2πr^2$	$\frac{2}{3}πr^3$

Maths – Circles, Arcs and Sectors

A **chord** (dashed line) divides the circle into two segments: a minor segment and a major segment.
NOTE: The diameter of a circle is the largest chord of that circle.

A chord also divides the circle into two arcs: a minor arc and a major arc.

This can be seen in the picture below.

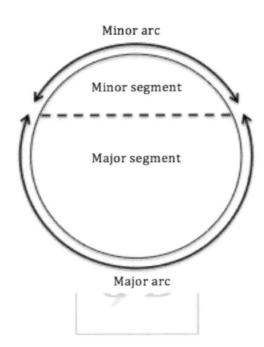

Minor arc

Minor segment

Major segment

Major arc

Length of an Arc
Consider the following diagram:

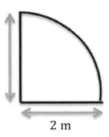

2 m

The arc is the curved part of the diagram. This arc is one quarter of a whole circle. Therefore, it length will be one quarter of the whole circle's circumference.

Diameter of circle = 2 x 2 = 4 m
Circumference = πd = π x 4 = 4π m
Length of arc = 0.25 x 4 = 1π m

To calculate any arc's length, you need to use the following formula:

$$\frac{Angle}{360} \times \pi \times d$$

Angle = Angle of the arc (in the example above, angle is 90°)
d = diameter of the circle

Area of a Sector

Two radii separate the area of a circle into two sectors as shown in the diagram below.

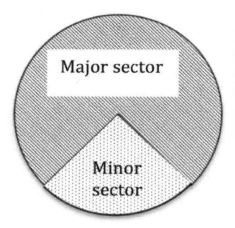

To calculate a sector's area, we need to know what fraction of a full turn the angle is.

We can use the same example we used in the arc section.

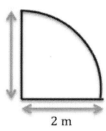

2 m

The angle is 90°. To find the area of this sector, we use the following formula:

$$\frac{!"\#\$\%}{90} \times$$

Maths - Similar Triangles

Two or more triangles are similar if they have the same shape but can be different sizes. How can we know if two triangles are similar?

We can know if triangles are similar if they can satisfy any one of the following conditions:

AAA (angle-angle-angle)

All three pairs of corresponding angles are the same.

AAA

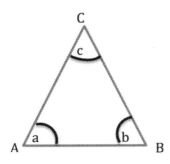
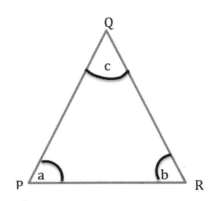

The Corresponding pairs of angles are:

$\angle ACB = \angle PQR$

$\angle ABC = \angle PRQ$

$\angle CAB = \angle QPR$

Therefore, these triangles are similar.

SSS (side-side-side)

All three sides in one triangle are in the same proportion to the corresponding sides in the other.

SSS

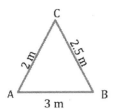
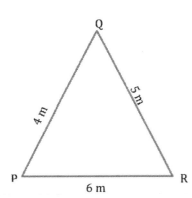

In the above triangles, the corresponding pairs of sides are:

(AC & PQ)

(CB & QR)

(AB & PR)

AC is half of PQ

CB is half of QR

AB is half of PR

All three corresponding pairs of sides are in the same proportion. Hence, the two triangles are similar.

SAS (side-angle-side)

Two corresponding pairs of sides are in the same proportion and the included corresponding angles are equal.

SAS

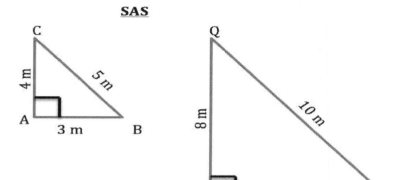

In the above triangles, the two corresponding pairs of sides are:
(AC & PQ)
(AB & PR)
The corresponding angles (∠CAB and ∠QPR) are equal.

AC is half of PQ
AB is half of PR
∠CAB = ∠QPR
Two corresponding pairs of sides are in the same proportion and the included angle is equal. Hence, the two triangles are similar.

Maths - Pythagoras Theorem

This theorem is only used for **right-angled triangles**.
In a right-angled triangle, there is always **one 90° angle** and the **sum of the other two angles is always to 90°**.

The side opposite the 90° is always the longest side. The longest side is called the **hypotenuse**.

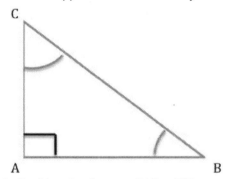

In the triangle above, ∠CAB = 90°

We know sum of all angles of a triangle = 180°
∠CAB + ∠ACB + ∠CBA = 180°
Since ∠CAB = 90°,
90 + ∠ACB + ∠CBA = 180°
∠ACB + ∠CBA = 90°

Since $\angle CAB = 90°$, the side opposite $\angle CAB$ (i.e. CB) is the hypotenuse.
According to Pythagoras' Theorem,
Hypotenuse² = (2nd side)² + (3rd side)²

Using the above triangle as an example, we can form the equation:
$CB^2 = AB^2 + AC^2$

If we have the value of AB and AC and we want to find the value of CB, we do the following:
$CB = \sqrt{(AB^2 + AC^2)}$

If we have the value of CB and AC and we want to find the value of AB, we rearrange to get the following:
$CB^2 - AC^2 = AB^2$
$AB = \sqrt{(CB^2 - AC^2)}$

If we have the value of CB and AB and we want to find the value of AC, we rearrange to get the following:
$CB^2 - AB^2 = AC^2$
$AC = \sqrt{(CB^2 - AB^2)}$

Pythagoras in 3-D Diagrams:

Question: Find the length of the black line in the following cube of side $3\sqrt{2}$ m.

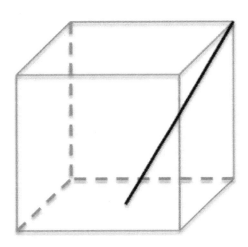

Solution:
You need to take into consideration that the black line is the hypotenuse of a right-angled triangle. The other two sides are: one edge of the cube, which is $3\sqrt{2}$ m and half of the diagonal of bottom face.

Length of diagonal of bottom face² = $(3\sqrt{2})^2 + (3\sqrt{2})^2$
Length of diagonal of bottom face² = 36 m
Length of diagonal of bottom face = 6 m

Half of the length of diagonal of one face = 3 m

Length of black line² = $3^2 + (3\sqrt{2})^2$
Length of black line ² = 9 + 18
Length of black line² = 27
Length of black line = $3\sqrt{3}$ m

Maths - Probability

Probability means how likely is an event going to occur. In maths, we can express the probability of something happening using either fractions or decimals.

A probability of 1 means that there is 100% chance of that event happening.

E.g. A bag contains only blue balls. Probability of picking a blue ball from that bag must equal to 1 since there is nothing in the bag besides blue balls.

Similarly, a probability of 0.5 or ½ means that the chance of something happening is 50%.

E.g. A bag contains 2 blue balls and 2 white balls. Probability of picking a blue ball from that bag must equal to 0.5.

No. of blue balls = 2

Total number of balls in the bag = 2 + 2 = 4

Probability = (2 ÷ 4) = 0.5 or ½

Example:

Julie wins a competition if she picks a red marble from a bag. The bag contains a total of 20 marbles. All marbles in the bag are either red or blue. The bag contains 12 blue marbles.

What is the probability of picking a red marble?

Solution:

We first need to find the number of red marbles in the bag. The bag contains only red marbles and blue marbles.

We know the number of blue marbles = 12

Total number of marbles in the bag = 20

So the number of red marbles in the bag = 20 − 12 = 8

Probability of picking a red marble = $^8/_{20}$ = $^2/_5$

Let us add a twist to the above question.

Julie manages to pick a red marble from the bag. The marble is not replaced.

She is told that if she picks another red marble, she can win double the prize.

What is the probability of picking a second red marble?

Solution:

The sentence "the marble is not replaced" is key here. "Not replaced" means that the marble that is picked already is neither placed back into the bag nor is it replaced with any other marble.

Therefore, total number of marbles in the bag now = 20 − 1 = 19

Since one marble is already picked, the number of marbles in the bag decreases by one.

Since a red marble was picked, the number of red marbles decreases by 1 too.

So number of red marbles = 8 − 1 = 7

Probability of picking a second red marble = $^7/_{19}$

Tree Diagrams

Tree diagrams are very helpful whilst solving probability questions.

Let us tweak the example above.

Julie wins a competition if she picks a red marble and a blue marble from a bag. The bag contains a total of 20 marbles. All marbles in the bag are either red or blue. The bag contains 12 blue marbles. Once a marble is picked, it is not replaced.

What is the probability of Julie winning?

Solution:
We know number of red marbles = 20 − 12 = 8

Order of picking one red marble and one blue marble could be:
– Red marble first and then a blue marble
– Blue marble first and then a red marble

Let us solve this by using a tree diagram.

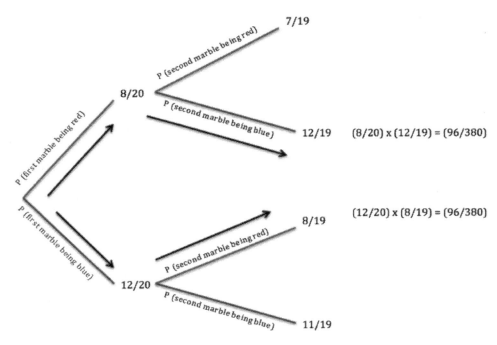

Probability of picking red marble first and then blue marble = $\frac{96}{380}$
Probability of picking blue marble first and then red marble = $\frac{96}{380}$

Julie could win if she does either of these possibilities.
Total probability of winning = $\frac{96}{380} + \frac{96}{380} = \frac{192}{380}$

Tree diagrams are easy to draw during exams if you are stuck. However, do not waste too much time as time is very limited during the exam.

Section 3 Introduction

What Is It?

In Section 3, you need to write an essay within 30 minutes. You will be given 3 options and you only need to answer 1 out of these 3 options.

How Is It Marked?

You are given a mark (1-5) on the quality of the content that you have written, with 5 being the highest mark. You can also get decimals such as 3.5 or 4.5. Quality of Content refers to the relevancy and importance of the points you have written. Your points and arguments must relate back to the question and should be written in an organised manner.

You are also given a grade (A- E) for your grammar, spelling and punctuation (basically how good your written English is). A is the best whilst E is the worst.
If you are able to write with good grammar and spelling, it is relatively easy to get an A.

Why I Think It Is the Easiest Section In The BMAT

Personally, I think that Section 3 is the easiest out of the three sections and there are mainly 3 reasons for this:

1) The time limit is more than enough to be able to finish the essay and proofread it 2-3 times.

2) There is no correct answer for this section. You write your own arguments!

3) If you safely address and answer all sub-questions in your chosen question, you can be confident that you will get a 3 or above, unless, you have written completely irrelevant points.
Be sure to read all the tips I have given in the following sections.

How Should You Prepare?

1) You do not need to write loads and loads of essays to practise. I would suggest you learn how to plan out Section 3 essays first. Planning skills are key in Section 3!

2) There are a total of 15 years of Past Paper Questions. This should be more than enough to help you improve your planning skills.

3) After you have finished planning each essay, go through its worked solution. Worked solutions may give you extra ideas of what your arguments could have contained.

4) Of course, you should practise writing full essays too. Try to do at least 10 essays before the exam at regular time intervals. Please ensure that you time yourself whilst you are doing the essay! Do them in an exam environment.

5) Do the practice essays in the answer sheet provided. You are not allowed an extra sheet in the exam, so you have to ensure that you fit all your arguments within that box on the specimen sheet. You **cannot** write anything outside the borders of the box.
I suggest you print out at least 10 sheets and write 10 full essays under exam conditions.

6) Here is what your timing should look like:

- **2-3 minutes**: Choosing the most appropriate question from the options given.

- **10-15 minutes**: Brainstorming ideas for the essays AND planning the structure of your essay.

- **10-12 minutes**: Once you have fully planned out your essay, it is time to write it out fully on the answer sheet given. Ensure that you do not make a huge mistake, which can cause you to scratch out everything, as you will not be given an extra sheet.

- **Last 1-2 minutes**: Proofreading

7) Lastly, do not think of Section 3 as a very big essay. Think of it like three or four paragraphs! For some reason, this helped me to become more confident and positive about Section 3.

Presenting Arguments

1) In your planning phase, brainstorm ideas for both arguments and list all the possible points that you can discuss. However, do not mention all the points in the actual essay.

2) Pick out the best points that you can discuss in detail. You must also take into consideration how much space you have given yourself for each argument on the answer sheet.

3) Relevancy is an important part of the essay. Ensure that you have chosen the points, which are pertinent and appropriate to the question.

4) Do not repeat your points again and again! This will not get you more marks. This is why it is important to choose a point, which you can discuss in detail.

5) Do not list 6-7 different points! It is essential that you provide 'Quality over Quantity'.

6) Do not repeat the same words or phrases such as 'however', 'furthermore' or 'whereas'.
It is better to improve your vocabulary and use some synonyms instead such as 'on the other hand', 'in addition to that' and 'together with this'.

7) Use examples where you can to support your arguments and give more weight to them. However, be careful! Do not use examples, which are irrelevant to your points and the question. This will only waste the limited space you have on the answer sheet.

Giving Balanced Arguments

1) Again, I would like to highlight the importance of choosing your points wisely. In order to give a balanced argument (which is a must in the BMAT exam), for every point you make, there must be a relevant counterargument.

2) Do not present your own views and thoughts in the middle of the essay. You should use facts and statistics that you know are correct and relevant to the argument. However, do not make things up!

3) Try and avoid using phrases, which highlight your point of view.
E.g. 'I (personally) believe', 'In my point of view' or 'I strongly believe that'
You can use some of the following words or phrases in your essay:

Transitional Words and Phrases	Agreement	Disagreement	Conclusion
Therefore	In addition to that	On the other hand,	Overall
Thus	Moreover	On the contrary	In conclusion
Hence	Furthermore	Others may argue that	To conclude
As a result,	Together with this	In contrast	

4) It is also essential that you read up on the Past Paper Worked Solutions to help give you ideas about what they could ask you on the exam.

How Can You Do Badly?

It is sometimes important to know how you can do badly in an exam rather than how you can do well and I think that Section 3 is a prime example of this.

1) Not answering all sub-questions.

"The only moral obligation a scientist has is to reveal the truth.

What is the reasoning behind this statement? Present an argument to the contrary.
To what extent do you agree that the only moral duty a scientist has is to reveal the truth?"

In the above question, there are three sub-questions:
a) What is the reasoning behind this statement?
b) Present an argument to the contrary.
c) To what extent do you agree that the only moral duty of a scientist has is to reveal the truth?

It is important for you to answer all the sub-questions. If you do not, you can only get a maximum of 2 marks for content.

2) Writing something completely irrelevant to the topic

3) Using poor grammar/punctuation and having many spelling errors

4) Misinterpreting the question or topic

If you are confident that you are not going to make the mistakes outlined above, you can be sure that you will get a decent score.

How to Get 4s or 5s?

Here is the real question. Since BMAT is a very competitive exam, everyone wants to get the top score in every section.

1) Answer all sub-questions of course.

2) Use nice language and relevant terminology.

3) Write down as many points as you can whilst you are planning and pick the best 1-2 points. Explain your best 1-2 points **in detail** instead of writing 4-5 points and not explaining them in detail.

4) Have good organisational skills. Most (if not all) questions ask you to write arguments 'For' and 'Against' a topic and then ask you to write out a Conclusion.

Write a paragraph for your 'For' argument, a separate paragraph for your 'Against' argument and a separate paragraph for your Conclusion.

Split your writing area into three to four sections by making small marks at the side before writing anything. When you put pen to paper, fit your paragraphs within those three to four sections. This is what an answer sheet looks like:

https://www.admissionstesting.org/Images/341346-bmat-nl-specimen-section-3-response-sheet.pdf

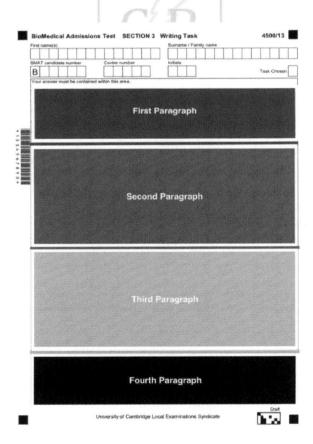

Just Some Final Tips

- You DO NOT need to use complex and sophisticated language! You will not be given extra marks for using long and fancy words. Just using simple language can help you get that A in Section 3.

- Use a variety of short and long sentences. However, do not use VERY long sentences in your essay. This can confuse the examiner and make your point unclear, lowering your mark for content. Therefore, if you feel like your sentence is very long, break it up into two or more sentences.

- You do not need to define any scientific terms you use. This will just be a waste of space. Use the space only to make arguments and present your points (Not for defining words).

- Use examples to support your arguments and ensure that these examples are relevant. I would suggest you read up on the issues regarding NHS and the 'trending' news in the medical field. However, don't push yourself too much.

- As I have mentioned before, do not make it very obvious to the examiner about your viewpoint. For your conclusion, never say 'I think' or 'I believe that'. Instead, use the terms and phrases mentioned in the 'Useful Words and Phrases.'

- DO NOT make up facts and figures in the exam. Some universities may bring up your essays during the interviews and if they ask you where you got your information from, you will be in trouble. Avoid using false information!

Section 3 Topics That You Can Gather Knowledge About

1) Knowledge About Human Body

This includes the different systems of our body (digestive system, circulatory system etc.) and structure of animal cells.

2) Genetic Disorders

- What are genetic disorders?

- How does an individual get a genetic disorder?

- Are they preventable or curable?

- Examples: cystic fibrosis and sickle cell anaemia.

3) Prevalent Diseases

Read up on diabetes, cancer, high blood pressure, heart disease and stroke. Don't go too much into detail. They will not ask you to give information about the disease. However, there is no harm in having some basic knowledge about such conditions.

4) The Daily Life of A Doctor

- What do they do?

- What kind of patients do they have to deal with?

- Should they have the right go on strikes? – You can read up on the **junior doctors strike** as this a good example to use if a question regarding strikes comes up.

---

5) Data protection and patient privacy

- Why is it bad to share a patient's information without their consent?

- Why is patient consent important?

- How old do you have to be to be able to give consent?

- What happens if you are not old enough?

---

6) NHS

- What problems is the NHS facing in terms of resources?

- Why is there a shortage of doctors and medical staff?

- What measures are being taken to solve the problems faced by the NHS?

- Is the NHS facing any financial problems? – Can you get some recent statistics?

---

7) 4 Pillars of Ethics

- What are they?

- How are they used?

- 1st is Autonomy → respect for patient's right to self-determination

- 2nd is Beneficence → the duty to 'do good'

- 3rd Non-Maleficence → the duty to 'not do bad'

- 4th is Justice → to treat people all equally and equitably

- How can you use these 4 pillars in your essay?

---

8) Ethics:

- What kind of ethical dilemmas do doctors face? E.g. euthanasia, medical errors, resource allocation (which department should receive more investment) etc.

- Should self-inflicted conditions be treated under the NHS? Do some reading on self-inflicted conditions and get arguments for and against this topic.

9) Animal Welfare:

- What rights do pets have?

- Should pets be given free healthcare under the NHS or is it the owner's responsibility to provide healthcare for their pet?

- Can you name some animal welfare organisations and state what they do? E.g. Word Animal Protection, RSPCA etc.

- The importance of pet health insurance

Again, there is **no guarantee** that these topics will come up in the exam. However, some preparation is better than no preparation. Therefore, I suggest you just read up on these topics as this knowledge may help you out in the future.

Most importantly, just do the planning phases of as many past paper questions as you possibly can. The planning phase only takes 10-12 minutes for each essay.

Then read as many Section 3 Worked Solutions as you can. This will only take a maximum of 1-2 hours, but I assure you that it will be worth it.

How many new doctor per year?
9 each year
7000 more
in 2021

10 Sample Essays

The following essays are past paper worked solutions. You can find the questions online on the Cambridge Assessment website. Try doing the essays on your own (At least the planning bit) and then look at these worked solutions.
For more worked solutions like these, please purchase the Crack BMAT Past Paper Worked Solutions (2003-2018) Book from Amazon.

2005 Section 3 Essays

1) The statement is not necessarily saying that animals do not feel physical pain as humans do. The word 'feel' can be used for emotional pain too. Therefore, the statement can be interpreted, as animals do not feel emotional pain in the same way as us.

Now, we cannot determine how much pain an animal is suffering from. Pain is a sensation that only an individual can feel. (Therefore it is difficult to answer the second question).

We can surely understand if an animal is feeling pain, either emotional or physical. It is often observed that a dog becomes depressed when they do not see their owners for a long time. They tend to eat less and can often be seen sitting in one area waiting for their owners to return. We can therefore argue that some animals do feel emotional pain. Humans also feel a similar kind of emotional pain when we lose someone really close to us.

If physical pain is inflicted on an animal, they try to escape or retaliate. These behaviours can hence help to argue against the statement.

It is impractical and unreasonable to think that all animals have the same nervous systems. Therefore, others may argue that some animals may not feel pain since they have a different brain physiology. They may not have the part of the brain that we have that senses pain.

---

2) Pronouncements sounds very similar to announcements (which mean to declare something). Pronouncement actually means a formal or authoritative declaration. Therefore, pronouncements in sciences would refer to any evidence or findings that have been obtained as a result of studies and researches, which have been declared authoritatively. In the second part of the statement, Sir James Jeans tries to convey the message that many scientific pronouncements have been proven wrong.

The most famous biomedical pronouncement that was proven to be false was the link made between MMR vaccines and autism by Andrew Wakefield. This link was later debunked by science as no research or study could prove that MMR vaccines were linked with autism. This pronouncement, however, caused lots of parents to refuse the MMR vaccination for their children. This resulted in many deaths due to measles, mumps and rubella.

This case highlights the importance of taking precautions before making an official biomedical pronouncement.

Others may argue that without pronouncements, we would not have the technology that we have now. Take the case of Dr. Edward Jenner, the father of immunology. His research involved exposing people to cowpox (which was harmless) to immunise them against smallpox. If Dr. Edward Jenner had not pronounced his findings and evidence, our knowledge of vaccines would not be possible. Similarly, Sir Alexander Fleming would not have discovered antibiotics.

Making pronouncements may motivate other scientists and doctors to follow in the footsteps of the likes of Dr. Edward Jenner and Sir Alexander Fleming.

3) The population of the world is ever growing and has been doing so for hundreds of years. As a result, the number of patients, as expected, is increasing proportionally. The statement is trying to say that with shortage of resources, doctors' main concern in the future would be whether to provide treatment or not. The doctors must then make decisions about who requires the treatment more.

The most obvious factor, which will contribute to the increasing demand, is the growing population. This occurs when the birth rate exceeds the death rate. Due to overpopulation, there will be shortage of food supply, which will cause malnourishment on a wide scale. These people will require immediate medical attention. Similarly, the amount of pollution, whether it is air, noise or water, will increase. This will lead to people being affected by diseases such as lung cancer, cholera or typhoid. The resources required to treat an increasing number of patients will fall short. Such resources include medical tools, machinery (such as X-ray machines or MRI) and even the medical workforce.

Others may argue that a doctor 'should always act in a patient's best interests'. Denying a treatment to a patient will certainly not uphold this statement. This would be opposing the very principle of the NHS. Refusing a treatment because someone else needs it more can be considered as passive euthanasia.

There are a lot of ethical and moral issues with this situation. The government can play an important role in ensuring cost-effectiveness in the medical field. Equal consideration should be given to all patients no matter their condition.

2006 Section 3 Essays

1) For Knowledge (not part of the essay):
zeal means enthusiasm
anthem in this statement means success
epitaph in this statement means failure

In this statement Bryan is trying to say that our constant desire and enthusiasm to make things better will lead not our success but to our failure. Since this statement was made with reference to modern technology, I think Bryan is trying to say that technology has more disadvantages than advantages.

Certainly, technology has made our lives much easier and more comfortable. Some of the things that we are now capable of include: use of vehicles for transport, contact someone thousands of miles away in seconds, access the internet and increase farm produce using advanced machinery.

However, this has reduced our capability to do more manual work. More comfortable lives have led to an increase in diseases such as obesity and diabetes. The trend of a fast paced lifestyle is spreading. This causes people to suffer from stress, high blood pressure and mental health issues.

The use of technology such as vehicles and industrial machinery produces large amounts of carbon dioxide which is a greenhouse gas and contributes to global warming. Global warming is a major world issue which is causing the climate change. This will ultimately lead to the extinction of many species of animals and plants.

On the other hand, advancements in technology have allowed us to provide much safer and faster medical treatments. The invention of the electron microscopes allowed us to study life at the molecular level. We were then able to study DNA and how the cells of the body work together to keep us alive. X-rays and MRIs have enabled us to provide non-invasive treatments. Being able to look inside the body without surgery is truly remarkable. This has reduced chances of complications and treatments going wrong.

The most effective way to tackle the disadvantages of technology is to use technology only when we need it. Also, we can use renewable sources of energy to limit carbon dioxide emissions and bring global warming under control. Proper treatments should be provided for those who suffer from sever stress and blood pressure problems. The use of machinery in agriculture has allowed us to provide food supply for the growing world population.

Space exploration for all humans can also be made possible in the coming years, allowing us to find new habitable planets.

Our reliance on technology has increased over the years and without it, we would be unable to do a number of daily tasks. In my opinion, it would be impractical to think that we can stop the use of technology completely.

---

2) In this statement, Nietzsche is trying to say that higher education is not compatible with a greater number of students. According to Nietzsche, the word 'higher' in 'higher education' indicates that only those who are exceptional in academics should be allowed to continue higher education.

Higher education in today's world usually means going to university to get a degree. The government tries to ensure that every student gets equal opportunity to go to university. Based on merit, the university may or may not select a student for a particular course. However, it is ensured that every student in A levels has a right to at least apply for a place in university.

Higher education is different from further education. In the United Kingdom, further education is compulsory until the age of 18. Schooling is compulsory until the age of 16. After the age of 16, individuals may take up A levels or do vocational courses in colleges. Higher education, on the other hand, is optional and students who want to have careers in medicine, dentistry, law, business etc. need to take higher education.

Some people may argue that the ratio of number of students and lecturers is too great. These lecturers often feel overworked which is not ideal, as they have to teach hundreds of students everyday. Therefore, Nietzsche may be right in the sense that universities right now are overcrowded and the students there may not be as intelligent or talented.

Other may debate that many students just view higher education as a way to have a career and lead a comfortable life in the future. This certainly is inarguable and every person wants to have a secure life. Even though they may not be academically strong as other students in their group, they have a right to study whichever subject they wish to study if they meet all the required criteria to be enrolled in that course.

It may be possible to provide higher education for a large proportion of the population by opening more universities and higher education institutions. There should be sufficient staff to allow students to get ample support and guidance so that no one feels left out or isolated. This will also prevent staff members from feeling stressed and overworked. Since there has been a rise in tuition fees, this extra money can be used to provide students with all the facilities that they require throughout their higher education journey. This will allow the students to improve intellectually and academically.

---

3) The statement is trying to say that if a patient has given permission for a treatment and if the treatment does not go according to the plan, then it is not the doctor's fault.

There is a limit to how true this statement is. If the treatment has gone wrong due to the carelessness of a doctor, then it must be their responsibility. If a treatment was going well and an unexpected event caused the treatment to go wrong, then the doctor should not be blamed for this. A treatment always involves a team of medical staff, ranging from doctors to nurses.

The principle of consent is an important part of medical ethics. It must be voluntary, informed and the patient must be capable of giving the consent. The consent can be given either verbally or in writing.

A meaningful consent is one in which the clinician provides all the details of the treatment. This includes all the procedures, length of procedures, side effects, and possible complications and how their life would be after the treatment. This way, the patient can truly decide whether to accept the treatment or not. This respects their autonomy and is one of the benefits of patient consent.

The patient must be in the right state of mind and must be fully informed before a treatment can be given. Only the patient can give the consent and this consent must not be given due to pressure from the medical staff, friends or family. In some cases, parents may need to give consent for a child up to the age of 16. Consent is not meaningful when a patient gives it due to pressure placed on them by medical staff, family or friends.

Clinical decisions should be made after the patient and their family have been fully consulted. The junior doctors must also consult a senior doctor. This will ensure whether the treatment being given to the patient is ideal or not. Once all the possible treatments have been discussed and the patient has given consent, the treatment can be started.

Ultimately, if patients have been fully informed about the treatment, complications, side effects and procedures, then it is their wish if they want to continue on with the treatment.

2007 Section 3 Essays

1) With this statement, Sigerist is trying to say that new technological advancements in medicine are being rejected by certain parts of society. There could many reasons for this e.g. cultural or personal beliefs.

Our technology has allowed us to carry out blood transfusions with ease. However, Jehovah's Witnesses refuse any treatments that involve blood transfusion from one person to another. There are many ethical and legal issues involved in a situation where a patient, whose condition is life threatening, is refusing a blood transfusion. The physician may be in a dilemma. In such a case, GMC's rule "make the care of your patient your primary concern" may contradict its other rule "you must respect a competent patient's decision to refuse an investigation or treatment, even if you think their decision is wrong or irrational".

The use of embryonic stem cells is also rejected by some people as it involves destroying an early embryo which means potentially destroying a human life. On one hand, you can help treat diseases like diabetes but on the other hand, you are destroying human life. There is much controversy regarding this.

To address such problems, scientists, doctors and researchers must find new methods of solving ethical problems such as the ones mentioned above. Researchers have been studying ways to obtain embryonic stem cells without interfering with the life of the embryo. In order to tackle the problem of blood transfusion, doctors have looked towards methods such as cell salvage and vasoconstriction. Together with this, erythropoietin is used which stimulates red blood cell production for patients who are in need of blood transfusion due to anaemia.

Alternatives to such treatments must be found so that the rule "make the care of your patient your primary concern" is upheld.

---

2) Our intense medical researches and studies have enabled us to provide treatments, which defy nature and have increased our life expectancy. This 'revolution' in medicine has changed our lifestyles and causes us to look at life and death from a different perspective.

These researches have not only allowed us to treat diseases but to also prevent them. Immunisation techniques are used to prevent people from being infected to dangerous diseases such as malaria or typhoid. These diseases were responsible for countless deaths before their vaccines were introduced. Other than this, the introduction of chemotherapy has cured many cancer patients. Even though cancer at its most dangerous level is not curable yet, we can still manage to save patients who have cancer at an early stage.

However, there are many negatives associated with longevity. Longevity is causing an imbalance between birth rate and death rate, resulting in overpopulation, which is an unwanted situation. This overpopulation puts pressure on the limited resources that we have such as land and water. The trend of famines, droughts and poor quality of life is increasing in many parts of the world today. This also puts pressure on the government to provide free treatments for the increasing number of people suffering from medical conditions. Some may argue that the ageing population, which is a result of longevity, may also be seen as a burden on medical resources.

Attitudes towards life and death have also changed drastically after the 'revolution'. People are now more ensured that they will be able to recover if their medical condition deteriorates. The trend for carrying out dangerous activities such as skydiving and bungee jumping is increasing. Such activities may have been deemed ridiculous hundreds of years ago.

On the other hand, other may argue that longevity has not really shaken the foundations of societies. Our fears of falling fatally ill still exist even though we have treatments and vaccines. We still view death as something unwanted and scary. Longevity has not changed our normal behaviour and way of life. We still need basic necessities such as food and water to survive.
People in third world countries still suffer from many problems so we cannot definitely say that their attitudes have changed towards life and death like people from first world countries.

---

3) This is a statement, which relates to epistemology. This basically means a theory of knowledge with regards to its validity.
Let us break down the statement. "Irrationally held truths" means something that is probably factual but lacks proof. It lacks proof that this truth is based on evidence and hence, cannot be justified. By "reasoned errors", Huxley is trying to say that if an individual has wrongly reasoned something, their logic is open to review for other researchers and scientists who can correctly give the accurate reasoning.

Huxley, in this statement, is trying to convey the message that 'something that is probably factual but lacks evidence' is more dangerous than 'something that is wrongly reasoned but is open to criticism'.

With regards to medicine, there are and have been many cases where the treatment given to a patient lacked evidence to prove that it is effective. Homeopathy is classic example of this. It is widely regarded as 'natural medicine', mainly in the eastern part of the world. They are not yet proven to be effective by science. However, some people do claim that it has worked for them and hence, should work for everyone. Such claims could prove to be fatal for some patients. Homeopathy can probably just have a placebo effect on some people but it is not necessary that it will do the same on others. Therefore, some may argue that it is inappropriate to treat someone with a serious illness with homeopathy since there is no evidence that it is effective.

The contrary argument could be that 'it is better to arrive at the correct answer without any method or incorrect method than to arrive at a wrong answer using the correct method'. This would be preferable in many cases in medicine. Some would argue that it is better to treat a patient with an invalid method with little evidence if no valid treatments work for them.
An example of this is the Deep Brain Stimulation to treat Parkinson's disease. Even though we do not know the exact mechanism behind this treatment, we can see positive results in patients. Therefore, the argument here is that as long as treatments repeatedly produce positive results on patients, we do not really need to know how they work.

In order to turn something irrational to rational, scientific researches need to be carried out. This allows evidence to support any claim. The work of many scientists in the past had been disregarded because there were other 'explanations' for the phenomena occurring around us e.g. religious explanations. However, later on, those works of scientists were later found to be true using rigorous and logical scientific experiments and studies.

2008 Section 3 Essay

1) The statement made by Lord Kelvin is suggesting that any qualitative knowledge that cannot be quantified is not sufficient, as knowledge should have both qualitative and quantitative aspects.

This applies to medicine and biology quite well. Whilst doing experiments in school, we make a link between an independent variable and a dependent variable. We then measure the dependent variable using apparatus such as a stopclock, measuring cylinder or water baths. This way, we obtain quantitative data to prove our hypothesis. Without the results, we would not be able to provide sufficient evidence for the link that we made between the independent variable and the dependent variable.

A good example of this is the yeast experiment to measure the rate of respiration. We use a stopclock to measure the time taken for methylene blue to change colour. We can then use the times to calculate the rate of respiration. In medical treatments, the use of blood reports is important for the identification of certain conditions. We need to quantify the RBC count, platelets count etc. to be able to recognise the condition a patient is suffering from.

However, we are still unable to quantify many results in medicine. This mainly applies for psychiatric disorders such as depressive disorders, neurodevelopmental disorders and personality disorders.

Printed in Great Britain
by Amazon